Discovering Data Mining
From Concept to Implementation

PETER CABENA ■ PABLO HADJINIAN ■ ROLF STADLER
JAAP VERHEES ■ ALESSANDRO ZANASI

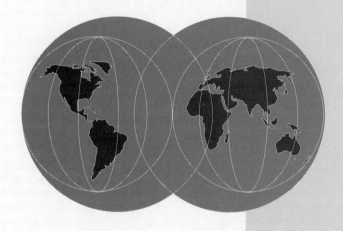

PRENTICE HALL PTR, UPPER SADDLE RIVER, NEW JERSEY 07458

Library of Congress Cataloging-in-Publication Data

Discovering data mining: from concept to implementation / Peter
    Cabena ... [et al.].
        p.   cm.
    Includes bibliographical references and index.
    ISBN 0-13-743980-6
    1. Data mining. 2. Marketing--Data processing. 3. Business--Data
processing.   I. Cabena, Peter.
HF5415. 125.D584   1997
658' .05631--dc21   97-18170
                                                             CIP

For information about redbooks:
http://www.redbooks.ibm.com/redbooks

Send comments to:
redbooks@vnet.ibm.com

Published by Prentice Hall PTR
Prentice-Hall, Inc.
A Simon & Schuster Company
Upper Saddle River, NJ 07458

Editorial/Production Supervision: James D. Gwyn
Acquisitions Editor: Michael E. Meehan
Manufacturing Manager: Alexis R. Heydt
Marketing Manager: Stephen Solomon
Cover Design Director: Jayne Conte
Cover Designer: Bruce Kenselaar

Prentice Hall books are widely used by corporations and government agencies for training, marketing, and resale.
The publisher offers discounts on this book when ordered in bulk quantities. For more information, contact: Corporate Sales
Department, Phone: 800-382-3419; FAX: 201-236-7141; E-mail: corpsales@prenhall.com; or write: Prentice Hall PTR,
Corp. Sales Dept., One Lake Street, Upper Saddle River, NJ 07458.

Printed in the United States of America

10 9 8 7 6 5 4 3

ISBN   0-13-743980-6

Prentice-Hall International (UK) Limited, *London*
Prentice-Hall of Australia Pty. Limited, *Sydney*
Prentice-Hall Canada Inc., *Toronto*
Prentice-Hall Hispanoamericana, S.A., *Mexico*
Prentice-Hall of India Private Limited, *New Delhi*
Prentice-Hall of Japan, Inc., *Tokyo*
Simon & Schuster Asia Pte. Ltd., *Singapore*
Editora Prentice-Hall do Brasil, Ltda., *Rio de Janeiro*

Dedicated to an unknown editor who rejected the idea of a book on data processing, ca. 1957, saying: *I have traveled the length and breadth of this country, and talked with the best people in business administration. I can assure you on the highest authority that data processing is a fad and won't last out the year.*

Contents

Figures

Foreword

Data mining is an interdisciplinary field bringing together techniques from machine learning, pattern recognition, statistics, databases, and visualization to address the issue of information extraction from large databases. The genesis of the field came with the realization that traditional decision-support methodologies, which combine simple statistical techniques with executive information systems, do not scale to the point where they can deal with today's larger databases and data warehouses within the time limits imposed by today's business environment. Data mining has captured the imagination of the business and academic worlds, moving very quickly from a niche research discipline in the mid-eighties to a flourishing field today. In fact, 80% of the Fortune 500 companies are currently involved in a data mining pilot project or have already deployed one or more data mining production systems.

While "data mining" refers to the use of methods that can automatically extract information from data with little or no user intervention, the term has become so popular that it now refers to other types of data analysis such as query and reporting, online analytical processing (OLAP), and statistical analysis. While not strictly synonymous, these methods are complementary to discovery-driven analysis techniques and in most real-world applications are used cooperatively. In particular, these methods are used to validate previously hypothesized business knowledge. Discovery-driven analytic methods are used to identify new business knowledge and to automatically refine previously validated knowledge. The in-depth study of the data mining techniques presented in this book will greatly assist the reader in making these distinctions.

Data mining, much like data warehousing, is driven by applications. The majority of these applications are aimed at understanding behavior; more specifically, comprehending customer behavior: how to acquire, retain, and increase the profitability and lifetime value of a customer. In addition, data mining applications help organizations understand whether a customer is involved in transactions that heighten various types of risk such as liquidity and fraud. Understanding the role of data mining techniques in the successful implementation of such applications is very crucial. In this book the role of data mining techniques is addressed through a series of case studies derived from systems developed by industry consultants.

Even in this early age of data mining, a common driver for applying such techniques is the availability of a large data set. Organizations are beginning to realize that they analyze only a relatively minute percentage of the data they capture and store on a daily basis. However, mining data only because one has a large data set is usually met with failure. An application domain and a process are necessary. The application domain provides the context for navigating through the process. In particular, the process (described in detail in the book) prescribes: 1) ways for determining which data will need to be mined, that is, identification of the appropriate data sources; 2) means for deciding on the granularity of each selected type of data, that is, determining which data will be used after being summarized and which data must remain in its most elemental form; 3) techniques for preprocessing the data and which techniques to select for data mining; 4) which tools in addition to data mining will have to be used to achieve the stated goals; and 5) how to interpret the results of the mining operations and select the information that will subsequently be used in decision making. Carefully identifying the application and following a well-articulated knowledge discovery process consistently lead to successful projects, as the book's authors confirm.

Data mining systems have quickly progressed from single-component tools to multicomponent toolkits with loose connections to database management systems. Next generation systems will be tightly integrated with the database management system and thus be capable of mining data in the database. However, increased sophistication of such systems will not automatically result in the success of the organizations using them. Organizations will need to assess whether they are ready for the application of such techniques. First, they have to establish the quality of their data. Although data mining techniques can be tolerant of certain types of noise, excessive noise will impact the quality of the mined information and in certain instances will even prohibit any meaningful mining. Second, organizations have to develop methods for establishing how and when to apply the appropriate techniques and determining how to best take advantage of the mined information. For example, organizations today attempt to improve their sales by trying to identify micro-markets through the application of data mining techniques. They become enamored with the fact that they can automatically identify hundreds, and at times even thousands, of segments (each perceived as a potential micro-market) through the use of clustering techniques, failing to address whether they can indeed successfully market to so many potential markets given their particular organizational infrastructure. In fact, the selection of the appropriate data mining tool should be the last step in this assessment process rather than the first step.

How do we know that the application of data mining methods has met with success? This is a hard question whose answer is often domain- and/or organization-dependent. Certain organizations estimate success through return on investment metrics. For example, a direct mail organization may estimate the return on its investment based on the response rate of the customers who were targeted through data mining methods and the overall cost of the particular campaign. In other organizations such "hard" metrics do not exist. In such instances we look at the degree with which organizations adopt data mining in their everyday operations. In the most successful of these organizations, data mining is used the way e-mail is used. Business analysts arrive every morning, log on to their computers, and bring up the data mining system to view the results of the overnight mining runs, in the same way they bring up their e-mail system to view the messages that have arrived overnight. They then begin making decisions based on the information presented to them by the data mining system.

Because data mining has been demonstrably successful within a short time, the expectations about the potential of the entire field have further increased. The newness of the field means that there is still a lack of appropriate resources to reduce the risk of failure for the newcomers. These resources include textbooks, data analysis methodologies, criteria for selecting data mining methods, techniques for selecting the most "interesting" and appropriate patterns from the data mining run, and guidelines for the interpretation and selection of results. There is significant need for resources that address the basic issues organizations will encounter as they use data mining; data quantity, and technology alone will not suffice. With this book the authors provide one rich resource to allow organizations to begin to educate themselves about the fundamentals of data mining, obtain answers to questions regarding the application of data mining methods, and learn from the successes and failures of a group of early adopters.

Evangelos Simoudis
Vice President
Global Business Intelligence Solutions
IBM North America

Preface

Thank you for picking up this book and taking the time to browse through the opening pages. Now that we have your attention, let us tell you a little about the book and the team that wrote it.

This book, like many before it, was written to fill a gap—a gap in the widening spectrum of material that is available on the topic of data mining. At one end of the spectrum, there is the growing coverage of the topic in popular trade magazines and on the Internet. At the other end, there is a vast array of highly technical and academic documentation from research centers and universities around the world.

This book is for all those who need something a little deeper than the popular sources but are not yet ready for the more technical or academic works. The book will appeal to a number of different types of reader, whether they simply want to be able to hold an informed conversation on this new and exciting topic or have just been entrusted with introducing data mining into their organization. Above all, this book is intended for newcomers to data mining, and it carefully avoids any use of complex mathematical or statistical details. It can be easily read by IT managers and many business managers with an IT interest or background.

How This Book Is Organized

This book is organized as follows:

❑ *Part 1, Introduction*

Intended for all readers, Part 1 introduces the basic concepts behind data mining and reviews the major uses of the technology today to solve real-world business problems.

➤ Chapter 1, *Data Mining: the Basics*

This chapter reviews the business and technical drivers for data mining, defines data mining, and positions it within the overall framework of data-driven approaches to solving business problems.

➤ Chapter 2, *Down to Business*

This chapter describes the major business areas where data mining is being applied today. It offers several real-world examples to support the general descriptions and concludes with come cautionary notes about the potential dangers in data mining applications.

❏ *Part 2, Discovery*

Part 2 is for readers who want a good understanding of what actually happens during data mining, how the algorithms work, and how to assess vendor solutions for data mining.

➤ **Chapter 3, *The Data Mining Process***

This chapter covers the process of data mining in detail. It introduces a phased, generic process, describing the objectives of each phase, who does what, the sort of things that can go wrong, and some hints and tips on how to avoid them. A real-world example is carried through the chapter to illustrate the points made.

➤ **Chapter 4, *Face to Face with the Algorithms***

Intended for the technical reader, this chapter introduces a general framework for describing the various data mining algorithms. Each algorithm is discussed in detail, including its general characteristics, strengths, and weaknesses.

➤ **Chapter 5, *Evaluating Vendor Solutions***

This chapter offers a general review of what readers should look for when they are assessing vendor solutions for data mining. The chapter covers data mining tools and data mining applications and services.

❏ *Part 3, Implementation*

Part 3 focuses on implementing data mining, first by describing what others have implemented and then offering advice on how readers can get started themselves.

➤ **Chapter 6, *Case Studies***

This chapter describes two real-world case studies in data mining. The discussion covers in detail the objectives of the mining project, the approach (including screen shots) taken by the data mining team, and the project results.

➤ **Chapter 7, *Getting Started with Data Mining***

This chapter is effectively a self-assessment checklist for readers who want to get started now with data mining. It starts with a review of the major challenges in data mining, offers advice on project selection and likely costs, and concludes with some critical success factors for data mining projects.

❏ *Appendixes*

➤ **Appendix A, *IBM's Data Mining Solution***

➤ **Appendix B, *Special Notices***

➤ **Appendix C, *Further Reading and Resources***

About the Authors

Peter Cabena is a data warehouse and data mining specialist at International Business Machine's (IBM's) International Technical Support Organization (ITSO), San Jose Center. He holds a Bachelor of Science degree in computer science from Trinity College, Dublin, Ireland. He has been extensively involved in the IBM data warehouse effort since its inception in 1991. In recent years, he has taught and presented internationally on the subjects of data warehousing and data mining.

Peter conceived and managed the project that produced this book and is its lead author. He can be reached by e-mail at Peter_Cabena@vnet.ibm.com.

Pablo Oscar Hadjinian is a data mining specialist in IBM's Banking Finance and Securities Industry organization in Buenos Aires, Argentina. He holds a Master of Science degree in computing science from the University of Alberta, Canada, where he focused his research on artificial intelligence (knowledge representation and reasoning). Pablo's Master's dissertation is entitled "Belief Revision in Logical Databases." At IBM he has helped banks manage customer relationships through the use of both data mining and data warehousing technologies.

He can be reached by e-mail at hadjinia@vnet.ibm.com.

Rolf Stadler is a senior systems engineer in the Banking Solution Center, IBM Switzerland. Since joining IBM in 1988 he has worked mainly in the areas of workflow and data management and on several major customer data warehouse and data mining projects.

Rolf can be reached by e-mail at rolf.stadler@ch.ibm.com.

Dr. Jaap Verhees is a data mining specialist in IBM's Global Business Intelligence Solutions Organization (GBIS) in The Netherlands. He holds a Ph.D. in Economics; his dissertation is entitled "Econometric Analysis of Multi-Dimensional Data Analysis Models." With IBM, Jaap has several years of experience in both data warehousing and data mining, assisting several of IBM's client organizations to plan and implement data-driven solutions.

Alessandro Zanasi is a data mining and data warehousing specialist at IBM's Bologna Data Mining Center. He graduated from the University of Bologna with a degree in Nuclear Engineering. Before entering IBM he worked at the University of Bologna, at the Carabinieri Scientific Investigations Center in Rome, and as an information broker. Following a four-year internship at IBM's Center for Applied Mathematics in Paris, he has consulted and lectured extensively as a business intelligence specialist around the world.

Alessandro can be reached by e-mail at zanasia@vnet.ibm.com.

Acknowledgments

This book would not have been possible without the help of an extended team. Among the long list of contributors, some names have a special place in the history of this book. For their help, advice, and encouragement throughout this endeavor, many, many thanks to Mike Channon, Dr. Bruce Fogarty, and Philippe Muller.

Thanks also to the following for their invaluable help in reviewing early drafts and/or contributing material: Rakesh Agrawal; Andreas Arning; Chuck Ballard (IBM's Visual Warehouse in "IBM's Data Mining Solution" on page 141); Dr. Joe Bigus (description of neural clustering in "Face to Face with the Algorithms" on page 61); Avijit Chatterjee (IBM's Parallel Visual Explorer in "IBM's Data Mining Solution" on page 141); Suzanne Dirks; Gerhard Henkel; Armand Herscovici; Dr. Charles Huot (IBM's Text Navigator in "IBM's Data Mining Solution" on page 141); Dr. George John (most of the figures in "Face to Face with the Algorithms" on page 61); Russ Lee; Christoph Lingenfelder; David Martin; Hammou Messatfa; Bernice Rogowitz (IBM's Diamond in "IBM's Data Mining Solution" on page 141); Dr. Michael Rothman; Riccardo Rucco (risk management applications in "Risk Management Applications" on page 30); Amit Seth; Dr. Richard Sharman; Dr. Evangelos Simoudis (Foreword); Betty Thana; and Dr. Alex Zekulin (original materials for "The Data Mining Process" on page 41).

A special thanks to the Health Insurance Commission of Australia and to Mellon Bank for their kind permission to use their names and details in the case studies. Specifically, thanks to Simon Hawkins (Health Insurance Commission) and Peter Johnson (Mellon Bank) for their participation.

Finally, thanks to the production team: Thomas Bilfinger, Maggie Cutler, James Gwyn (Prentice Hall), Barbara Isa, Evelyn Jackson, Michael Meehan (Prentice Hall), Marissa Stairs, Marisa Viveros, and Amy Voge.

Peter Cabena

Peter Cabena

Comments Welcome

We want our redbooks to be as helpful as possible. Please send us your comments about this or other redbooks in one of the following ways:

❑ Use the electronic evaluation form found on the Redbooks Home Pages at the following URLs:

For Internet users

    http://www.redbooks.ibm.com

For IBM Intranet users

    http://w3.itso.ibm.com/redbooks

❑ Send us a note at the following address:

    redbook@vnet.ibm.com

Your comments are important to us!

Part 1
Introduction

1

Data Mining: the Basics

The key to success in business is to know
something that nobody else knows.
(Aristotle Onassis)

Back to the Future

It was 1956. Mr. Miller worked in a small hardware store on the corner of Elm and Main streets. The family had owned and lived over the store as long as anyone could remember. In fact, as a schoolboy, Mr. Miller used to work behind the counter during summer vacation. The store was known for miles around. Of course, it wasn't the *only* hardware store in town—but it was the *best*. For a small store it surely packed in a lot. No matter what a customer needed, Mr. Miller seemed to be able to produce it from somewhere in the shop. Somehow he could always recall what had worked well for any specific customer the last time they had called in. In fact, sometimes Mr. Miller seemed to know more about what his customers needed than they knew themselves, such as the type of replacement light bulb that Mrs. Garcia needed when her faulty hall light was giving her trouble again. The whole town will always remember the Sunday afternoon when Dr. Grossman's new automobile broke down right outside the store. It must have taken the doctor and Mr. Miller most of the afternoon to get the machine going again, by which time most of the town, and most of Mr. Miller's shop, was lined up on Main Street!

Of course, by today's standards, Mr. Miller was operating in a very simple environment. Those were the days before mass production and mass media and the inevitable offspring of those two great forces—mass marketing. People's buying patterns and behavior remained relatively static over long periods of time simply because the main determinants of behavior—preferences, perceptions and availability of choices—did not change very frequently. Price was not an issue. New competitors were unlikely to enter into the limited marketplace in the small town. Thus Mr. Miller could build up a loyal set of customers and a level of intimacy with them that would be the envy of any commercial organization today, large or small. Mr. Miller never heard of customer relationship management, share of customer, customer lifetime value, or 24x7 operations, yet he inherently knew their value and practiced them instinctively. He knew his customers well enough to predict what they wanted even when they did not know themselves. He knew his high-spending customers but he made time for everyone because he also knew the lifetime value of a good and loyal customer. His common sense told him that because his share of market would always remain limited to the immediate area, he had to concentrate on share of customer, rather than share of market. In this way he could ensure that his existing customers bought *all* of their hardware from him and felt little need to shop elsewhere.

The traditional, one-to-one customer relationships which Mr. Miller enjoyed do not come easily today. Fundamental changes in society and industry have ensured that this is the case. Traditional customer relationships have largely disappeared. Consumer behavior is infinitely more volatile in an environment of quickly changing demographic and psychographic patterns.

Today, more and more organizations are realizing the value of getting back to a more intimate relationship with their customers. These organizations are seeing a rejuvenation in their customer relationships as a vital weapon in the battle to attract new customers, or just to retain existing ones. What once came for free now has to be worked on, one customer at a time. For these organizations, movement towards closer customer relationships is a critical first step on the road back to the future.

Why Now?

Much of the current upsurge of interest in data mining arises from the confluence of two great forces: the need for data mining (drivers) and the means to implement it (enablers). The drivers are primarily the business environment changes which have resulted in an increasingly competitive marketplace. The enablers are mostly recent technical advances in machine learning research, database, and visualization technologies. This happy coincidence of growing commercial pressures and major advances in research and information technology lends an inevitable push toward a more advanced approach to informing critical business decisions.

Before looking at these drivers and enablers in some detail, it is worth reviewing the commercial backdrop against which these two forces are coming together.

Changed Business Environment

Today's business environment is in great flux. Fundamental changes are influencing the way organizations see and plan to approach their customers. Among these changes are:

❑ **Customer behavior patterns**

Consumers are becoming more demanding and have access to better information through buyers' guides, catalogs, and the Web. New demographics are emerging: Only 15% of U.S. families are now traditional single-earner units, that is, a married couple with or without children where only the husband works outside the home. Many consumers are reportedly confused by too many choices and are starting to limit the number of businesses with which they are prepared to deal. They are starting to put more value on the time they spend shopping for goods and services.

❑ **Market saturation**

Many markets have become saturated. For example, in the U.S., almost everyone uses a bank account, has at least one credit card, has some form of automobile and property insurance, and has well-established purchasing patterns in basic food items. Thus, in these areas, there are few options available to organizations wishing to expand their market share. If a merger or take-over is not possible, such organizations often must resort to effectively stealing customers from competitors—often by what is called predatory pricing. Lowering prices is not a sound long-term strategy, however, as only one supplier can be the lowest-cost provider.

❑ **New niche markets**

New, untapped, markets are opening up. Examples are the handicapped and ethnic groups which are seen as having a very distinct set of requirements that must be addressed in a special way, or the current U.S. inner-city hip-hop culture, which is seen as an avenue to the more lucrative suburban consumer market where the trends in clothing and music take longer to emerge. Highly specialized stores are emerging. For example, SunGlass Hut has 1,600 stores around the world selling nothing but, you guessed it, sunglasses—literally thousands of different styles.

❑ **Increased commoditization**

Increased commoditization, where even many leading brand products and services are finding it increasingly difficult to differentiate themselves, has sent many suppliers in search of new distribution channels. Witness the increase in online service outlets, from catalogs to banking and insurance to Internet-based shopping malls. Suppliers are increasingly asking, Who are my customers and how best can I reach them?

❑ **Traditional marketing approaches under pressure**

Traditional mass marketing and even database marketing approaches are becoming ineffective, as customers are increasingly turning to more targeted channels. Customers are shopping in fewer stores and are expecting to do more one-stop shopping.

❑ **Time to market**

Time to market has become increasingly important. Witness the recent emergence and spectacular rise of Netscape Communications Corporation in the Web browser marketplace. With only a few months' lead over its rivals, Netscape captured an estimated 80% of the browser market within a year of establishment. This is the exception, of course; most companies operate by making small incremental changes to services or products to capture additional customers.

❑ **Shorter product life cycles**

Today products are brought to market quickly but often have a short life cycle. This phenomenon is currently exemplified by the personal computer and Internet industries where new products and services are offered at arguably faster rates than at any other time in the history of computing. The Chairman of IBM, Lou Gerstner, recently coined the phrase "web year" as a synonym for three months, when referring to this quickened pace. The result of these shortened life cycles is that providers have less time to turn a profit or to "milk" their products and services.

❑ **Increased competition and business risks**

Many of the above changes tend to combine to create a climate which is significantly more competitive and a more challenging risk management environment for many organizations. General trends like commoditization, globalization, deregulation, and the Internet make it increasingly difficult to keep track of competitive forces, both traditional and new. Equally, rapidly changing consumer trends inject risks into doing business that were never there before.

Drivers

Against this background, many organizations have been forced to reevaluate their traditional approaches to doing business and have started to look for ways to respond to changes in the business environment. The main requirements driving this reevaluation are:

❑ **Focus on the customer**

The requirement here is to rejuvenate customer relationships with an emphasis on greater intimacy, collaboration, and one-to-one partnership. In turn, this requirement has forced organizations to ask new questions about their customers and potential customers, for example:

➢ What general classes of customer do I have? Are there recognizable sub-populations within the customer base who have similar behavioral patterns and needs and who may be open to targeted marketing messages?

➢ How can I sell more to my existing customers? Who among them will be more likely to buy additional products or services from me?

➢ Is there a recognizable pattern in which my customers acquire products or use services so I can market to them just-in-time?

➢ Which of my customers will prove to be good, long-term valuable customers and which will not? Are there customers who are costing me money?

➢ Can I predict which of my customers are more likely to default on their payments or to defraud me so that I can begin to contain my rising bad debt costs?

❑ **Focus on the competition**

Organizations need to focus increasingly on competitive forces with a view to building up a more modern armory of business weapons. Some of the approaches to doing this are:

➢ Prediction of potential strategies or major business plans by leading competitors, for example, the opening of a new line of business or territory.

➤ Prediction of tactical movements by local competitors, for example, the opening and location of new outlets, price changes, or new service offerings.

➤ Discovery of sub-populations of existing customers that are especially vulnerable to competitive offers.

❑ **Focus on the data asset**

There is a growing awareness among business and Information Technology (IT) managers that there is currently an information-driven opportunity to be seized. Many organizations are now beginning to view their accumulated data resources as a critical business asset.

Some of the factors contributing to this growing awareness are:

➤ Growing evidence of exponential return on investment (ROI) numbers from industry watchers and consultants on the benefits of a modern corporate decision-making strategy, based on data-driven techniques such as data warehousing. Data mining is a high-leverage business where even small improvements in the accuracy of business decisions can have huge benefits. Figure 1 on page 9 illustrates the ROI from 62 actual data warehousing implementations.

➤ Growing availability of data warehouses. As the data warehouse approach becomes more pervasive, the early adopters are forced to leverage further value from their investments by pushing into new technology areas to maintain their competitive edge.

➤ Growing availability of success stories, both anecdotal and otherwise, in the popular trade press.

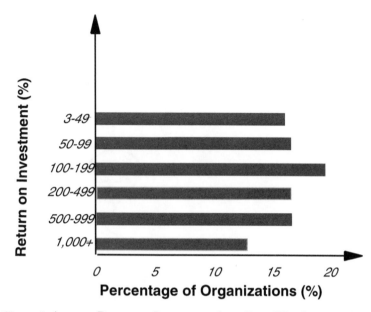

Figure 1. *Average Return on Investment from Data Warehousing Projects*
Source: DCI, "The Foundations of Wisdom: A Study of the Financial Impact of
Data Warehousing, 1996."

Figure 2 on page 10 attempts to summarize the situation. The frustrated business executive is attempting to grasp new opportunities such as better customer relationships and improved services. He fails, however, given the combination of a rapidly changing business environment and poor or outdated in-house technology systems.

Enablers

There is a set of enablers for data mining which, when combined with driving forces listed above, substantially increases the momentum towards a revised approach to business decision making:

❑ **Data flood**

Forty years of information technology have led to enormous amounts of data (measured in gigabytes and terabytes) being stored on computer systems. Computerization of daily life has caused data about individual behavior to be collected and stored by banks, credit card companies, reservation systems, and electronic points of sale. A typical business trip today generates an automatic electronic audit trail of a traveler's habits and preferences in airline travel, car hire, credit card usage, reading material, mobile phone services, and perhaps Web sites.

Figure 2. *New Customer Relationships Out of Reach*

Of course, much of this data is collected to run the business (to plan reservations and bill customers), but increasingly it is being exploited to manage the business (track trends and discover new opportunities). For example, from transaction data at an electronic point of sale, one can find interesting correlations between the items being purchased at the same time. These correlations can be used for target marketing or for conducting promotional campaigns.

In addition, the increasing availability of demographic and psychographic data from syndicated providers, such as A.C. Nielsen and Acxiom in the United States, has provided data miners with a useful data source. The availability of such data is particularly important given the focus in data mining on consumer behavior, which is often driven by preferences and choices that are not visible in a single organization's database.

❏ **Growth of data warehousing**

The growth of data warehousing in organizations has led to a ready supply of the basic raw material for data mining: clean and well-documented databases. Early adopters of the warehousing approach are now poised to further capitalize on their investment. See "The Data Warehouse Connection" on page 18 for a detailed discussion of the integration of data warehouse and data mining approaches.

❏ **New information technology solutions**

More cost-effective IT solutions in terms of storage and processing ability have made larger-scale data mining projects possible. This is particularly true of parallel technologies, as many of the data mining algorithms are parallel by nature. Furthermore, increasingly affordable desktop power has enabled the emergence of sophisticated visualization packages, which are a key weapon in the data mining armory.

❏ **New research in machine learning**

New algorithms from research centers and universities are being pressed into commercial service more quickly than ever. Emphasis on commercial applications has focused attention on better and more scalable algorithms, which are beginning to come to market through commercial products. This movement is supported by increasing contact and joint ventures between research centers and commercial industries around the world.

The net effect of the changed business environment is that decision making has become much more complicated—problems have become more complex and the decision making process less structured. Decision makers today need a set of strategies and tools to address these fundamental changes.

Toward a Definition

It is difficult to make definitive statements about an evolving area—and surely data mining is an area in very quick evolution. However, we need a framework within which to position and better understand the subject. Figure 3 shows a general positioning of the components in a data mining environment.

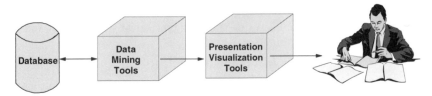

Figure 3. *Data Mining Positioning*

Although there is no one single definition of data mining that would meet with universal approval, the following definition is generally acceptable:

> **Data Mining...**
>
> is the process of extracting previously **unknown**, **valid**, and **actionable** information from large databases and then using the information to make crucial **business decisions**.

The highlighted words in the definition lend insight into the essential nature of data mining and help to explain the fundamental differences between it and the traditional approaches to data analysis such as query and reporting and online analytical processing (OLAP). In essence, data mining is distinguished by the fact that it is aimed at the discovery of information, without a previously formulated hypothesis.

First, the information discovered must have been previously **unknown**. Although this sounds obvious, the real issue here is that it must be unlikely that the information could have been hypothesized in advance; that is, the data miner is looking for something that is not intuitive or, perhaps, even counterintuitive. The further away the information is from being obvious, potentially the more value it has. (Remember what Aristotle Onassis had to say at the beginning of this chapter!) Data mining can uncover information that could not even have been hypothesized with earlier approaches. The classic example here is the anecdotal story of the beer and diapers. Apparently a large

...in of retail stores used data mining to analyze customer purchas-
... patterns and discovered that there was a strong association
...etween the sales of diapers and beer, particularly on Friday evenings.
...t appears that male shoppers who were out stocking up on baby requisites for the weekend decided to include some of their own requisites
at the same time. If true, this shopping pattern is so counterintuitive
that the chain's competitors probably do not know about it, and the
store manager could profitably exploit it. However, if a car retailer
uses data mining on his historical sales records, only to discover that
large sedans are bought primarily by older, wealthy customers, he is
probably not going to gain much commercial benefit. Although this
purchasing pattern was unknown to this particular retailer, his competitors most likely knew about it.

Second, the new information must be **valid**. This element of the definition relates to the problem of overoptimism in data mining; that is,
if data miners look hard enough in a large collection of data, they are
bound to find something of interest sooner or later. For example, the
potential number of associations between items in customers' shopping baskets rises exponentially with the number of items. Some
chains carry upwards of 300,000 items, so the chances of getting spurious associations is quite high. The possibility of spurious results
applies to all data mining and highlights the constant need for post-
mining validation and sanity checking.

Third, and most critically, the new information must be **actionable**,
that is, it must be possible to translate it into some business advantage. In the case of the retail store manager, clearly he could leverage
the results of the analysis by placing the beer and diapers closer
together in the store or by ensuring that the two items were not dis-
counted at the same time. In many cases, however, the *actionable* criterion is not so simple. For example, mining of historical data may
indicate a potential opportunity that a competitor has already seized.
Equally, exploiting the apparent opportunity may require use of data
that is not available or not legally usable. Needless to say, an organization must have the necessary political will to carry out the action
implied by the mining.

The ability to use the mined data to inform crucial **business decisions** is another critical environmental condition for successful commercial data mining, and underpins data mining's strong association
with and applicability to business problems.

Revolution or Evolution?

Given the current level of hyperbole surrounding the subject, the new-comer to data mining may well be tempted to believe that a revolution is under way. The short historical review that follows will show, however, that data mining is much more evolutionary than revolutionary.

Very early in the history of electronic data processing, computers caught the imagination of mathematicians and researchers as a means of automatically making decisions. Advances in research quickly spawned the idea of machine learning—the notion that a computer, fed with a number of observations about known, solved cases, could develop a general set of underlying rules that were universally true. In human terms, this notion can be compared to a newcomer trying to write the book of rules for a game by simply watching it being played (according to the rules, of course). Picture yourself on the sidelines of a basketball or soccer game, making notes on the players' movements and the resulting scores or actions. Eventually, if you were to watch enough games, you could probably write the rules. We are not sure this is what was on the mind of Frank Rosenblatt when, in the early 1960s, he developed his now famous *Perceptron*, one of the precursors to modern neural networks. The Perceptron was limited in the types of problems it could tackle, however, and, despite great expectations at the time about its possibilities, this single-node neural network never went beyond solving simple problems. In 1969, after Minsky and Papert developed a more complex neural network architecture and thus exposed certain theoretical limitations in the Perceptron, research in this area waned in favor of a new approach—knowledge engineering.

Knowledge engineering is founded basically on the notion that, rather than asking a machine to work out the rules from observed experiences, the rules (or knowledge) are precoded and fed to the machine. This is equivalent to coding up the rule book and writing a program to consult it in an intelligent way. The early 1970s saw the development of several expert system applications, which again were hailed as having potential far greater than one could reasonably expect. Some examples of well-known expert systems are MYCIN (medical diagnosis) and XCON VAX (computer configuration). While interest in expert systems continued during the 1970s and 1980s, many critics saw them as not really reaching their full potential. Partially because of the often massive investment in time and effort to gather and maintain the formalized knowledge base and partially because of the limitations in the technology, expert systems were never developed to a level where they could seriously emulate real human experts.

Under these circumstances, by the mid-1980s the time was right for a revival in the machine learning approach, and a new batch of graduate students and researchers began to produce more advanced neural networks capable of solving more complex problems. This new generation of networks used such techniques as two layers of neurons and back propagation which were major advances over Rosenblatt's Perceptron. The new networks found widespread use in such areas as risk assessment scoring for marketing campaigns, and in 1987 the world saw the First International Conference on Neural Networks in San Diego, California. Also around this time, the rising interest in new machine learning was matched with an increase in the availability of large commercial databases. One of the most common approaches was to process large in-house and purchased databases to more accurately target marketing campaigns. Database marketing, as it was called, quickly established itself as the latest and greatest weapon in the armory of the mass marketeers.

By the end of the 1980s, a new term, *knowledge discovery in databases* (KDD), was coined to replace all of the old terms whose objective was to find patterns and similarities in raw data. Artificial intelligence and machine learning practitioners quickly adopted KDD and used it to cover the overall process of extracting knowledge from databases, from setting the business goal to eventual analysis of the results. In this context, the words *data mining* were used for the step in the process when the mining algorithms were applied. This interpretation was formalized at the first International Conference on KDD, which was held in Montreal in 1995. Recently, as a result of the increasing attention of vendors and the popular trade press in this area, the words *data mining* have been hijacked and have come to mean, like KDD, the overall process of extracting knowledge from databases. As this popular interpretation seems set to continue for some time, it is the interpretation we use throughout this book.

What's So Different?

This is possibly the most frequently asked question among newcomers to data mining, especially if they have a background in such areas as database marketing, traditional data analysis, or statistics. The reasons for the question are not hard to see given that data mining is most popularly used today for database marketing and is almost always used in conjunction with traditional data analysis techniques, including statistics. In addition, the situation is not helped by the current level of coverage in the popular trade press, nor by vendors who seek to position their tools to take advantage of the rising tide of interest in data mining.

Data mining is often thought of as one or more of the following: of:

- ❏ Structured Query Language queries against a large data warehouse
- ❏ SQL queries against any number of disparate databases or data warehouses
- ❏ SQL queries in a parallel or massively parallel environment
- ❏ Advanced information retrieval, for example, through intelligent agents
- ❏ Multidimensional database analysis (MDA)
- ❏ OLAP
- ❏ Exploratory data analysis (EDA)
- ❏ Advanced graphical visualization
- ❏ Traditional statistical processing against a data warehouse

None of these approaches is data mining because each lacks the essential ingredient—*discovery of information without a previously formulated hypothesis*. Review the list yourself quickly to prove the point.

A good rule of thumb is that, given the exploratory nature of data mining, whenever we know clearly the shape and likely content of what we are looking for, we are probably *not* dealing with a data mining problem. Figure 4 on page 17 illustrates this rule. Assume that the business user is a regional manager of a chain of consumer electronics stores. His query may well be to determine the volumes of video cassette recorders (VCRs) sold in one of the northern stores last month. He may use a graphics package to plot the recent history of different VCR sales per store over time. If he needs to analyze the price sensitivity of a new line of televisions when sold in the urban stores, he may use statistical regression. Finally, if he is comparing the sales of various products in different stores over time, he may well use an MDA tool. All of these scenarios have one thing in common: a hypothesis. The manager knows that there are stores, products and sales figures and he is simply checking out the interrelationships. Even in the price sensitivity analysis case, he hypothesized that there was, in fact, some sensitivity, before setting up the analysis. This is traditional data analysis and, clearly, it is a useful and essential part of managing any business today.

Data mining, however, raises the bar on what can be achieved by traditional data analysis. It does this by tackling questions that are beyond the reach of traditional techniques and, more importantly, have a far greater business value. In the example above, data mining would allow the regional manager to get answers to such questions as: Why are my discount coupons not attracting the sort of return I was expecting? How can I increase the share I have of my customers' total spending on electronic goods? How can I get my other stores to match the incredibly successful sales figures of the two northern branches?

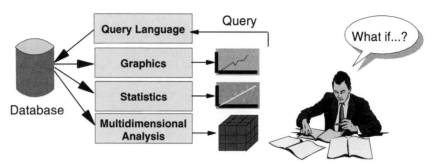

Figure 4. *Traditional Data Analysis, Not Data Mining*

Of all of the various techniques in traditional data analysis, statistics is closest to data mining, and it is worth spending a little time to better understand the relationships between the two. In fact, it is fair to say that statistics traditionally has been used for many of the analyses that are now done with data mining, such as building predictive models or discovering associations in databases. Indeed, for each of the major areas of data mining endeavor, there is a broadly equivalent statistical approach and it is probably true that much, if not all, of what is done in data mining *could* be done with statistics—eventually. What is attracting many analysts to data mining is the relative ease with which new insights can be gained (though not necessarily interpreted) in comparison to traditional statistical approaches.

The accessibility of data mining shows up in many ways. For example, data mining is always a hypothesis-free approach, whereas most popular statistical techniques require the development of a hypothesis in advance, and statisticians typically have to manually develop the equations that match the hypotheses. In contrast, data mining algorithms can develop these equations automatically. For example, models that attempt to predict customer behavior are essentially a set of such equations. Because of the additional manual effort in statistics, many analysts limit their use of some advanced statistical techniques such as nonlinear regression.

Recent research in machine learning has started to yield several new data mining algorithms that are especially suited to larger data volumes, and the emergence of these algorithms from the research labs has added to the commercial attractiveness of data mining.

Finally, the kind of data input that is acceptable also helps to explain some of the attractiveness of data mining. Whereas statistical techniques usually handle only numeric data and need to make strong assumptions about its distribution, data mining algorithms typically can process a much wider set of data types and make fewer assumptions about their distribution—or no assumptions at all.

In summary, there is no single factor which makes data mining an outright winner over traditional statistical approaches. Indeed, this is never the case, and statistics play an important and integral role in most data mining environments. Rather, although the distinguishing factors discussed here appear to favor data mining rather than traditional statistics, the optimal strategy is always to use statistics and data mining as complementary approaches.

Not So Different

Clearly then, data mining is no more or less than the latest in a long line of approaches to solving business problems through analysis of data. However, because of its fundamentally different approach and greater accessibility, it holds out the prospect of significantly improving the speed and quality of business decisions. Nevertheless, as a data-driven approach to business decision making, data mining inherits a key weakness of its predecessors, namely, a critical dependency on clean, well-documented data. Along with this dependency comes an overexposure to the most fundamental rule of all computing, namely, *GIGO (garbage in garbage out)*. This point is best illustrated by a true story of a data mining team in an insurance company that attempted to build a model to predict who among the company's clients would be most likely to have automobile accidents. The team took all of the data it had (demographic, behavioral, and so on) about the clients and discovered that the most useful variable for forecasting the tendency to be involved in a car accident was a client's zodiac sign! In fact, it appeared that people born under the sign of Pisces were most prone to accidents. Luckily, the conclusion was so suspicious that the team quickly checked its input data. Apparently, the vast majority of the clients just happened to be born under Pisces, so naturally the majority of accident victims would also be Pisces. What would have happened if the conclusion were taken at face value can only be imagined!

Data mining may make results more accessible, but it does not necessarily make them any easier to interpret.

The Data Warehouse Connection

Data warehousing, although a separate topic and practice from data mining, is nevertheless very closely associated with it. Thus it is worth reviewing the basics of data warehousing to help illuminate some of the linkages as well as some of the differences.

First, bear in mind that a data warehouse is not a prerequisite for a data mining solution. In fact, although data warehouses are one of the drivers of increased interest in data mining, much data mining today is done from flat files which have been extracted directly from operational data sources.

The Data Warehouse

The aim of a data warehouse is to help improve the effectiveness of data-driven business decision making. The concept is based fundamentally on the distinction between operational data (used to run the organization) and informational data (used to manage the organization). The data warehouse is designed to be a neutral holding area for informational data and is intended to be the sole source of quality company data for decision making. It is different from the operational data stores in a number of ways.

Inmon (1992) offers a well-accepted definition of a data warehouse.

> **A data warehouse...**
>
> is a **subject-oriented**, **integrated**, **time-variant**, and **nonvolatile** collection of data in support of management's decisions.

Subject-oriented The data in the warehouse is defined and organized in business terms, and is grouped under business oriented subject headings, such as customers, products, Sales Analysis Report, and Marketing Campaigns. This subject orientation is achieved through data modeling.

Integrated The data warehouse contents are defined such that they are valid across the enterprise and its operational and external data sources. For example, all occurrences of common data elements such as customer number and gender codes must be consistently represented to enable consistent reporting from the warehouse.

Time-variant All data in the data warehouse is time-stamped at time of entry into the warehouse or when it is summarized within the warehouse. Thus it acts as a chronological record and provides historical and trend analysis possibilities. Typically, operational data is overwritten in situ as past values are not of interest.

| **Nonvolatile** | Once loaded into the data warehouse, the data is not updated. Thus it acts as a stable resource for consistent reporting and comparative analysis. |

Many analysts and corporations view data warehousing as one of the most strategic vehicles for executive decision making. The Gartner Group estimates that upward of 90% of major organizations have or are building some kind of data warehouse. One of the most celebrated examples from the retail world is that of Wal-Mart in the United States, which captures information from its stores and analyzes the details of every line item to enable better merchandising decisions on a daily basis.

The Data Mart

Clearly, setting up a data warehouse is not a trivial task, especially if the aim is to service the entire enterprise. Thus in recent years many organizations have opted for the data mart, which is more specialized, more accessible, and a lot smaller than an enterprise-wide data warehouse. As such, it is an excellent first step for many organizations. For those organizations that already have full-blown data warehouses, a data mart is a useful device for specialized processing, for example, by a department or individual data analyst.

From Data Warehouse to Data Mine

The step from the data warehouse to the data mine is one that organizations with a progressive view of decision support systems are increasingly taking. The step is a natural one because:

❑ An organization that has already invested in a data warehouse knows the strategic value of the corporate data asset and is therefore well disposed to the concept of data mining.

❑ Much of the hard work in understanding, gathering, and cleaning the business data has already been done, so the organization is well positioned to further capitalize on its investment in the data warehouse.

The rationale for the move from data warehouse to data mine arises from the need to increase the leverage that an organization can get from its existing warehouse approach and the need to handle larger and larger data warehouse volumes (Wal-Mart is reported to be approaching 10 terabytes).

From Data Mine to Data Warehouse

After implementing a data mining solution, an organization could decide to integrate the solution in a broader data-driven approach to business decision making. The development of a data warehouse in this scenario has the following drivers:

❑ A successful data mining project will have demonstrated the strategic value of the corporate data asset, and thus focussed the attention of executive management on the validity of data-driven solutions.

❑ A data warehouse will provide an excellent vehicle for integrating the data mining solution into the business and technical infrastructure of the organization. An integrated data warehouse and data mining solution is a key part of a modern business decision-making infrastructure.

Data Mining and Business Intelligence

We use *business intelligence* as a global term for all of the processes, techniques and tools that support business decision-making based on information technology. The approaches can range from a simple spreadsheet to a major competitive intelligence undertaking. Data mining is an important new component of business intelligence. Figure 5 on page 22 shows the logical positioning of different business intelligence technologies according to their potential value as a basis for tactical and strategic business decisions.

In general, the value of the information to support decision-making increases from the bottom of the pyramid to the top. A decision based on data in the lower layers, where there are typically millions of data records, will typically affect only a single customer transaction. A decision based on the highly summarized data in the upper layers is much more likely to be about company or department initiatives or even major redirection. Therefore we generally also find different types of users on the different layers. A database administrator works primarily with databases on the data source and data warehouse level whereas business analysts and executives work primarily on the higher levels of the pyramid.

Note that Figure 5 portrays a logical positioning and not a physical interdependence among the various technology layers. For example, data mining can be based on data warehouses of flat files, and visualization techniques can be used outside data mining, of course.

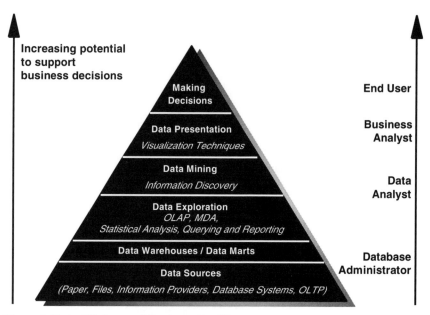

Figure 5. *Data Mining and Business Intelligence*

Where to from Here?

It is probably a little early to ponder the future of data mining, but some trends on the horizon are already becoming clear.

Data mining technology trends are becoming established as we see the scramble by vendors who seek to position their tools and services within the new data mining paradigm. This will be followed by the inevitable technology shakeout where some vendors will manage to establish leadership positions in the provision of tools and services and others will simply follow. Doubtless, new data mining algorithms will continue to be developed but, over time, the technology will begin to dissolve into the general backdrop of database and data management technology. Already, we are seeing the merging of OLAP and MDA tools and the introduction of SQL extensions for mining data directly from relational databases.

On the data mining process side, there will be more open sharing of experiences by the early adopters of data mining. Solid, verifiable success stories are already beginning to appear. Over time, as more of the implementation details of these successes emerge, knowledge of the data mining process will begin to move out into the public domain, in much the same way as has already happened with the data warehousing process.

The final phase in the evolution will be the integration of the data mining process into the overall business intelligence machinery, while the data mining technology will become more difficult to distinguish as a separate entity. In the long run, data mining, like all truly great technologies, may simply become transparent!

2

Down to Business

No one can possibly achieve real and lasting
success in business by being a conformist.
(J. Paul Getty)

In this chapter we provide general insight into the state of the art in data mining today, emphasizing real-life, commercially successful applications of the technology. In general, the discussion is at the business level and does not require a detailed understanding of the data mining process. Figure 6 on page 26 illustrates the three general business areas where data mining is applied today and lists some of the common applications in each area.

This short review is, by definition, limited in both its breadth and depth. We cover only a small selection of the representative, interesting, and accessible examples. In many of them, because of the sensitivity of most commercial data mining applications, we omit much of the fine detail.

The examples presented in this chapter are taken from several sources, including publicly available references and the files of IBM Global Services engagements, with the permission of the clients involved.

Market Management	Risk Management	Fraud Management
✔ Target marketing ✔ Customer relationship management ✔ Market basket analysis ✔ Cross selling ✔ Market segmentation	✔ Forecasting ✔ Customer retention ✔ Improved underwriting ✔ Quality control ✔ Competitive analysis	✔ Fraud detection

Figure 6. *Data Mining Application Areas*

Market Management Applications

Market management is one of the most well-established application areas for data mining. Perhaps the best known application area is *database marketing*. The objective is to drive targeted and therefore effective marketing and promotional campaigns through the analysis of corporate databases. In general, the sales organization builds a consolidated database of customer product preferences and lifestyles from such sources as credit card transactions, loyalty cards, warranty cards and discount coupons, entries to free prize drawings, and customer complaint calls. When mixed with publicly available information from sources such as lifestyle studies, this information forms a potent concoction. Data mining algorithms then sift through the data, looking for clusters of "model" consumers who all share the same characteristics—for example, interests, income level, and spending habits. Clearly this group is a target for marketing efforts. It is a win-win game for both the consumers and marketeers: Consumers perceive greater value in the (reduced) number of advertising messages, and the marketeers save by limiting their distribution costs *and* getting an improved response to the campaign.

Bank of America, the largest retail bank in the United States, uses database marketing to improve customer service, and profits. Like other banking institutions around the world, the bank has suffered a disconnection from its customers thanks to the advent of modern automated banking technology. With fewer customer visits to the bank, there is less opportunity to interact with customers and market and sell services. By consolidating five-year customer history records, Bank of America is now in a position to market and sell targetted services to the 100,000 customers who phone the bank every day.

Another application area for data mining is that of determining customer purchasing patterns over time. Marketeers can determine much about the behavior of consumers such as the sequence in which they take up financial services as their family grows, or how they change their cars. Commonly the conversion of a single bank account to a joint account indicates marriage, which could lead to future opportunities to sell a mortgage, a loan for a honeymoon vacation, life insurance, a home equity loan, or a loan to cover college fees. By understanding these patterns, marketeers can advertise just-in-time to these consumers, thus ensuring that the message is focused and likely to draw a response. In the long run, focusing on long-term customer purchasing patterns provides a full appreciation of the lifetime value of customers, where the strategy is to move away from share of market to share of customer. An average supermarket customer is worth $200,000 over his or her lifetime, and General Motors estimates that the lifetime value of an automobile customer is $400,000, which includes car, service, and income on loan financing. Clearly, understanding and cultivating long-term relationships bring commercial benefits.

The approach of focusing ever more closely on consumers as individuals with their own value sets, expectations, and habits, and seeing them as lifetime investments, is often referred to as *one-to-one marketing* or *marketing to a segment of one*.

Cross-selling campaigns constitute another application area where data mining is widely used. Cross selling is where a retailer or service provider makes it attractive for customers who buy one product or service to buy an associated product or service. Mellon Bank, a mid-sized bank in the United States, uses data mining to ensure effective and appropriate cross-selling of its products to existing customers. For example, the bank has used data mining to identify customers with demand deposit accounts who are likely to be interested in a home equity loan. It builds a model of customers who already have taken out a home equity loan of their own volition and uses the model to pinpoint other customers who may be interested in following suit.

Improved Catalog TeleSales

In the fall of 1995, RS Components, a United Kingdom-based worldwide distributor of high-quality technical products, started a project called *Opportunity Selling*. The project objective was to identify opportunities where telephone order clerks could inform customers of associated products they might also want to purchase.

The project has enabled the company to track the products its customers order most frequently as well as to suggest the purchase of those products in future orders. Whereas some product associations were obvious, such as soldering irons and solder, with as many as 66,000 items in stock, many of the relationships among highly technical products were not as apparent. The associations have been fed back into the operational system to enable prompting of potential additional sales. In addition, RS Components has used the associations to enable new startup branches to ramp up sales. In essence, the operational system has now captured the hidden intellectual property represented by the associations.

Sharper Customer Focus through Loyalty Cards

Retail stores are increasingly using loyalty cards, sometimes called *affinity cards*, to reward their frequent buyers. The underlying concept is that because cardholders get special treatment, such as exclusive discounts on selected items, they are thus encouraged to do more of their shopping at that store and are less likely to visit the competition. When loyalty cards were first started, store owners saw them more as a means of raising the brand image than promoting sales. However, many owners are now exploiting the information the cards provide for reasons that are well beyond the original purpose of the cards.

COIN, one of the most customer-oriented non-food retail chains in Italy, uses loyalty-card data to understand the kinds of customers who are shopping in their stores, with a view to better targeting store promotions. The store has consolidated its loyalty-card data with demographic details to segment the tens of thousands of customers into sub-populations.

Figure 7 shows a small sample of the actual results of the data mining by the COIN team and illustrates how the sub-populations of customers can be accurately identified and addressed. Because the two groups share some of the same characteristics, a cosmetics promotion, for example, could target the two groups as one, whereas a promotion of children's apparel would focus on group 1 only, and a seasonal promotion of gardening supplies would target group 18 only.

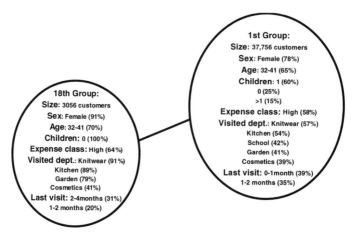

Figure 7. *Customer Segments with Similar Characteristics*

Turning External Influences to Advantage

In an effort to develop just-in-time marketing campaigns, a European life insurance company decided to use data mining to segment its customer base. The mining discovered two groups of clients who appeared at first sight to be very similar; for example, they had similar levels of income and savings, which were two of the key criteria for the segmentation.

At first, the company was tempted to merge the groups into one because of the similarities. However, historical analysis of the life insurance purchasing behavior of the two groups between 1988 and 1992 showed that when one group decided to invest, the other group decided to cash in its policies (see Figure 8). The reason for this variation in behavior was the different fiscal treatment each group received during the period: The fiscal policy changed twice in that period because of changes in government. The net result was that one group had much more to gain by investing a life insurance than did the second group. Under these circumstances one group was attracted by the higher risk, while the other was risk-averse. The insurance company now recognizes these two groups as quite distinct and has developed marketing strategies to capitalize on their different predicted behavior in the event of new fiscal policy changes.

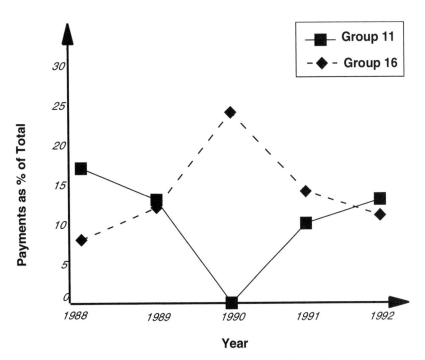

Figure 8. Different Investment Behavior Driven by Fiscal Treatment

Getting More Out of Store Promotions

ShopKo is a major regional discount chain in the United States with 129 stores in 15 states. Although the chain's Sunday circular advertising program, where inserts in Sunday newspapers offer discount coupons for selected items such as health and beauty products, was seemingly very successful, the company was looking for a better way of measuring the effectiveness of the campaign. Data mining of the point-of-sale data revealed that shoppers who were coming into the store were gravitating to the left side of the store for the promotional items and were not necessarily shopping the whole store. As a result, the chain added apparel, which was stocked on the right side of the stores, to the promotion and launched a similar midweek promotion. As a result, sales of all products, including apparel, increased.

Risk Management Applications

Risk management covers not just risk associated with insurance or investments, but also the broader business risks arising from competitive threat, poor product quality and customer attrition.

Risk is a core aspect of the insurance industry, and data mining is well suited to predicting property or casualty losses for policyholders. Such predictions are usually in the form of rules that support underwriters. In addition, understanding the total loss exposure more precisely can support improvements in the overall insured portfolio.

Variable pricing for insurance policies is one way in which insurers can address differences in financial risks associated with differences among policyholders. Another way is to target market to a segment of the customer base with a common risk level.

Attrition means the loss of customers, especially to competitors. Attrition is an increasing problem in an increasingly competitive marketplace, and data mining is used in the finance, retail, and telecommunications industries to predict likely customer losses. The general approach is to build a model of a vulnerable customer, that is, a customer who shows characteristics typical of one who is likely to leave for a competitive company. Analysis of recently lapsed customers often shows nonintuitive patterns. For example, customer losses may frequently follow a change of address or a recent protracted exchange with an agent of the company. One U.S. bank uses models such as these to predict the loss of customers up to one year in advance and is thus well positioned to take remedial action. Another U.S. bank analyzes more than one million credit card account histories to ensure that it is not overexposed to high rates of attrition.

Retail organizations use data mining to better understand the vulnerability of certain products to competitive offerings or changing consumer purchasing patterns. Historical purchasing patterns of customers are analyzed to identify groups of customer with low product or brand loyalty.

A classic application from the banking sector is in the area of credit scoring for loan application processing. Here a historic example of both good and bad loan histories is used to develop a profile of a good and bad new loan applicant. For example, applicants from a pool of existing customers with good track records with above-average salaries are more likely to be granted a loan than new customers with low salaries.

Data mining makes it possible for banks to segment loan customers into classes that are likely to show different failure rates and the factors responsible for the failures. Then, a class-based pricing procedure can provide the necessary spread to assure lenders that loans to customers in classes with higher failure rates would not in the long run yield less than loans to lower-risk customers.

U.S.-based telecommunications companies have several billion dollars in uncollectible debts every year, which represents a significant problem. For these companies, data mining can build models that help predict whether a particular account (or class of accounts) is likely to be collectible and is therefore worth going after.

An additional application area in the telecommunications industry is that of managing telecommunications networks. Information can be mined to establish patterns with a view to improving network reliability by proactively forecasting potential problem areas. Since 1992, AT&T has been using an application called *Scout* which continuously monitors its networks. Users of Scout have reported increased productivity because they can troubleshoot new problems faster.

Today, more than ever, it is vital for organizations to monitor their competitors and market directions. This increased focus on competition has given rise to the practice of competitive intelligence (CI), the process of collecting, analyzing, and disseminating information about industry developments or market trends to enhance a company's competitiveness.

One popular and reliable source of advanced technical information is international patent databases. It has been calculated that about 80% of important technical information appears first under a patent. As these patents are increasingly available in online databases, they are now more amenable to data mining technology. The principal disadvantage of these databases, however, is that they are large and complex. Patents and technical reports are often written in so specialized a language that they cannot be easily read or analyzed in relation to each other.

Some examples from the list of online technical databases are Chemical Abstracts, INSPEC, Medline, and World Patent Index Latest (WPIL). Figure 9 showsan extract from the WPIL database. Data mining provides an innovative solution for extracting useful information from these databases.

```
1/3881 - (C) Derwent Info 1994
AN : 94-364398 [45]
TI  : Television with function for enlarging picture by variation of
      deflect ion frequency - has microprocessor for controlling
      system synchronous signal output, horizontal and vertical
      frequency drive circuit, sync. signal counter, signal detector.
DC : W03
PA  : (GLDS ) GOLDSTAR CO LTD
IN  : HO J
NP : 1
PR  : 88KR-011143 880831
IC  : H04N-005/262; C08J-005/18; G11B-005/704
PN : KR940043 B1 940120 DW9445 HO4N-005/262 001/pp
AB : No abstract
```

Figure 9. *Patent Reference Extracted from an Online Database*

Forecasting Financial Futures

Finance is a discipline that has always been strongly interested in looking for ways of predicting the future, for several reasons:

❑ If changes in financial behavior can be predicted, the organization can adjust its investment strategy and capitalize on the predicted changes.

❑ There is agreement on the measure (money) to be used and its amenability to quantitative treatment.

❑ Early computerization provided a headstart for building up what are now massive databases.

The application of advanced quantitative techniques such as statistics and data mining in the area of risk management is often referred to as *financial engineering*. One example of a tool used in financialengineering is the financial "future," which is essentially a contract that allows someone to buy a commodity at a certain price on a certain date in the future. The "future" is a right to buy something and this right can be bought or sold for a price on the open market. The price will change according to the expected final price of the future.

Clearly, the ability to forecast the right price of a future is a challenging but rewarding job for which data mining applications are already available.

This application is used to predict the values of two financial futures on the Italian securities market. The prediction window is very narrow, no more than a few minutes in most cases, but can be sufficient to give the broker a competitive advantage.

A model is used to predict the future price changes. The historic price movement of the futures themselves along with several external, but related, influencing factors, constitute the key inputs to the model. The application revises its prediction every 10 minutes, according to the movement of various inputs over the previous several hours of trading. The prediction also indicates those external factors that could influence the predicted value in any way.

The predicted values are reliable for up to 10 minutes. Values are especially accurate for the first five minutes. Use of the predictions after several hours shows less reliable results.

Pricing Strategy in a Highly Competitive Market

REPSOL, a chain of gasoline stations in Spain, uses data mining to develop profitable pricing strategies in a very competitive and commoditized marketplace. The chain, which is owned by the FINA Oil Company, has developed a model that helps to determine daily optimal prices for its leading products and to predict the likely effects of potential price adjustments by its competitors.

From REPSOL's five geographically nearest competitors, the model takes such inputs as the competitors' recent prices for motor fuel (super, unleaded, and diesel), gas station facilities, supported methods of payment, and even the physical driving distances from the REPSOL station.

REPSOL uses the results from this and related models to show the sensitivity of profit levels to competitive change in any of the areas covered by the model and to predict:

1. Appropriate pricing for its products on a day-to-day basis, with a view to maximizing sales and profits

2. Sales volumes and profitability

3. The likely competitive reaction to REPSOL price changes

4. The likely profitability of new REPSOL stations

Fraud Management Applications

Human nature dictates that some level of fraud is inevitable in all industries. However, some sectors, notably those where there are many transactions, appear to suffer more than most. For this reason, many organizations in such areas as health care, retail, credit card services, and telecommunications are well advanced in their use of data mining to guard against fraud and potential fraud. The general approach is by now a familiar one: use historical data to build a model of fraudulent behavior or potentially fraudulent behavior and then use data mining to help identify similar instances of this behavior.

Telecommunications companies regularly use data mining to detect phone card fraud. A model is used to scan the millions of daily transactions in an effort to detect potential fraud. Some of the more important elements in building the model are the destination of the call, duration, and time of day or week. In this way, calling patterns that deviate from an expected norm can be analyzed for potential fraud.

Mellon Bank uses data mining to protect itself and its customers' funds from potential credit card fraud.

Fraud at POS terminals is another form of abuse that is amenable to data mining, given the ready availability of computerized sales transactions. Analysts estimate that 38% of retail shrink is due to dishonest employees.

Detecting Inappropriate Medical Treatments

Healthcare systems around the world are struggling to find ways to control rising costs. One proven way of keeping costs down is to ensure that all medical tests and services are appropriately prescribed and accurately billed.

The Australian Health Insurance Commission (HIC), an Agency of the Australian federal government, maintains computerized records of every doctor's consultation in the country, including details on the diagnosis, prescribed drugs, and recommended treatment.

Using traditional data analysis techniques, HIC had noticed a rapid increase in the number of prescribed pathology tests. HIC could identify the sources of the increase but it wanted to better understand the pattern of these pathology referrals. It was particularly interested in knowing whether these expensive tests were being prescribed in a consistent way, that is, consistently by all practitioners under the same circumstances. Data mining was used to identify which combinations of tests were commonly used. HIC identified that in many instances blanket screening tests were being requested as opposed to specific tests targeted at given symptoms. In addition, an invalid combination of tests was discovered where in many instances an inappropriate (and more expensive) test was requested.

Following this discovery, HIC enhanced its operation systems to detect these invalid combinations and to no longer accept them for benefit payment. HIC estimates that this action alone saved A$1 million in the first year of operation.

Detecting Telephone Fraud

British Telecom (BT), the traditional telecommunications provider in the United Kingdom, fights a constant battle against fraud. Fraudsters cost BT millions of dollars every year and range from single individuals to internationally organized gangs.

In early 1994 BT Security, a division of BT, started an investigation into potentially fraudulent calls to several premium rate information and entertainment services. Over a three-month period, some 360,000 premium rate call records were collected and analyzed, 20,000 of which were subsetted for more detailed study. Analysis of the call patterns clearly identified discrete groups of callers. These groups had an intra-group call frequency of more than 50% whereas they made no calls to other identified groups. Equally, some groups were linked by only a single pair of subscriber numbers. Call patterns of the mobile phone groups were particularly interesting.

After an analysis using data mining techniques, BT successfully prosecuted the perpetrators and broke a multi-million dollar fraud.

Emerging and Future Application Areas

The current intense interest in commercial data mining looks set to continue and will therefore guarantee an increasing list of new application areas. Presently, two of the developing areas are *text mining*, the application of traditional data mining technology to the unstructured contents of text databases, and *web analytics*, which proposes to use data mining technology in conjunction with the Internet.

Text Mining. The objective of text mining is not literary criticism (at least not yet); rather it is to make the ever-increasing volume of textual information amenable to rapid analysis and understanding. Typical early applications are the automatic indexing of documents and automatic patent analysis. Recently, text mining has been used at the University of Helsinki to analyze textual databases such asUsenet Newsgroups. The Helsinki work uses the technology to do a full-text scan of the document database and then produces a visual document map where similar or related documents are placed close together. The words are analyzed in context; for example, if the words *White House* appear in an article about architecture, the article is placed close to other articles about architecture, not politics.

Whereas traditional search engines are typically constrained by a literal word-matching approach and the inventiveness of the user, the text mining approach opens up the possibility of picking out information linkages that the user did not initially specify or even think possible. For example, mining the unstructured contents of customer letters of complaint may well reveal hidden fundamental problems with service or product quality that would not otherwise be visible.

Charles Schwab & Co., the largest provider of online brokerage services in the United States, makes extensive use of data mining, including text mining. For example, the company is introducing text mining techniques to automatically mine incoming customer e-mail to the call center. Responses are automatically prepared and resent without need for human intervention.

Although there is still much to be done in the area of text mining—for example, it is still not possible to intelligently summarize a children's story book—it is the target of much research at this time and several commercial products are likely to emerge in the near future.

Web Analytics. Web analytics bring together two of the biggest focus areas in computing today—the Internet and data mining.

The idea is to apply data mining to the activity logs of Web servers to develop insights into user behavior on the Internet. Today, Web hypertext links are typically fixed. The site developers have provided the most likely links by trying to second-guess what the user wants to do next. With data mining, historical user browsing patterns can be analyzed to dynamically suggest related sites for users to visit.

The obvious potential in this application of data mining has prompted several vendors to rush to market with commercial products and services.

When Things Go Wrong!

Despite all of the success stories mentioned so far, sometimes things *do* go wrong. Data mining without due regard for the business objectives, the data at hand, and basic common sense is not likely to lead to satisfactory results. The real-life accounts in this section help to demonstrate this point.

A Class of Divorced Women. When a large retail store applied data mining to look for hidden classes of customers among its loyalty card users, it made an interesting discovery: divorced women have distinctly different shopping patterns from those of either single or married women. The discovery looked like an excellent targetted marketing opportunity. Luckily, when the team went to validate its findings, it discovered what really happened. The data on marital status was much less accurate than the other data. Because of cultural norms, customers were reluctant to give such personal information, so out of a data set of more than 20,000 clients, only several hundred declared their marital status, and only some admitted to being divorced.

The class of divorced women was simply not statistically significant, so although the result was interesting, it was neither valid nor actionable.

Missing the Point. While preparing to mine a database of hospital patient admission records, a data analyst used some traditional visualization techniques to understand the cleanliness and distribution of the information. The analyst discovered an unexpected anomaly in the distribution of the temperature of the patients as recorded at the time of admission (see Figure 10 on page 38).

The anomaly was easily explained after some investigation. It appeared that the nurse at the admissions deck had shied away from recording patient temperatures that were exactly on the point of the well-known threshold for fever, that is, 37°C (98.6°F). A patient on the point of fever was likely to have his or her temperature recorded as either 36.9°C or 37.1°C.

Clearly, if this anomaly remained undetected, it would have introduced serious bias into the input data and potentially into the mining results. Happily, this was discovered before the mining run, and the biased distribution was adjusted.

The Strange Effects of Diet Drinks. Our final account is a classic case of confusing cause and effect.

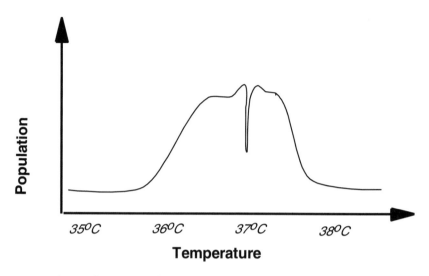

Figure 10. *Anomaly in a Population Temperature Distribution*

A common problem in clinical studies is that little or no data on historical dietary habits is available, although diet is clearly a key factor in many medical problems. Without historical data on which to base conclusions, data mining can be less than useful. Strong correlations in the data can often mask the presence of an unseen third factor, which is the real cause of the observed condition. This was highlighted by Piero Bonissone when he facetiously concluded that, based on observations, drinking diet drinks leads to obesity!

Part 2
Discovery

3

The Data Mining Process

Man is still the greatest computer of all.
(John F. Kennedy)

In this chapter we discuss the internals of the data mining process in detail to provide general insight into what happens during a typical data mining project. The chapter as a whole is aimed at the business and data analyst and the data management professionals who support them.

Before You Start

Because there is probably no such thing as a *typical* data mining project, the process described here is, by definition, generic. It has no dependency on any particular vendor, tool, or data mining application. As such, some details have been left out for the sake of clarity. Also, the process is not a panacea—simply following it will not necessarily guarantee success any more than knowing the recipe for your mother's famous homemade bread will guarantee a faithful reproduction of the original. In general, our discussion concentrates on the mechanics of the data mining process and makes only passing reference to such major environmental success factors as executive sponsorship and expectations management. "Critical Success Factors" on page 138 covers these latter points in more detail.

The Process in Overview

In general, when people talk about data mining, they focus primarily on the actual mining and discovery aspects. The idea sounds intuitive and attractive. However, mining the data is only one step in the overall process. Figure 11 illustrates the process as a multistep, iterative process.

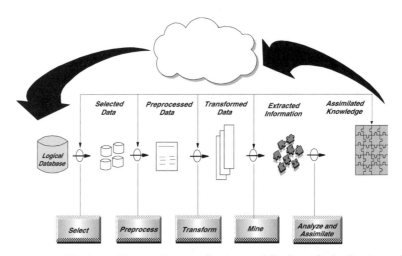

Figure 11. *The Data Mining Process: Begins and Ends with the Business Objectives*

The business objectives drive the entire data mining process. They are the basis on which the initial project is established and the measuring stick by which the final results will be judged, and they should constantly guide the team throughout the many steps in the process. Although the steps are performed in the order in which they are presented, the process is highly iterative, with possibly many loopbacks over one or more steps. In addition, the process is far from autonomous. In spite of recent advances in technology, data mining remains very much a labor-intensive exercise.

Speaking of labor-intensive, not all steps in the process are of equal weight in terms of typical time and effort spent. Figure 12 presents a broad outline of the steps in the process and the relative effort typically associated with each of them. As you can see, 60% of the time goes into preparing the data for mining, thus highlighting the critical dependency on clean, relevant data. The actual mining step typically constitutes about 10% of the overall effort.

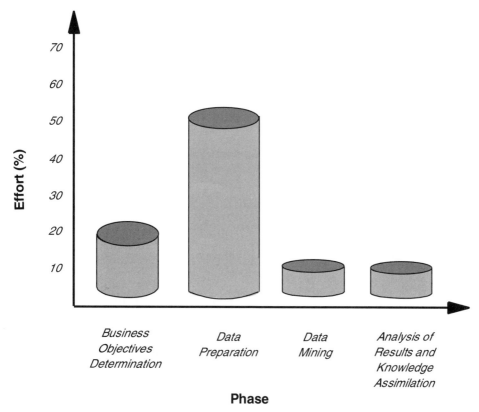

Figure 12. Effort Required for Each Data Mining Process Step

In overview, the steps are:

Step 1: Business Objectives Determination

Clearly define the business problem or challenge. This is an essential ingredient in any data mining project. Although it sounds intuitive and straightforward, it is not. Data mining for the sake of data mining (and it does happen) is rarely successful.

Step 2: Data Preparation

Step 2.1: Data Selection

Identify all internal or external sources of information and select which subset of the data is needed for the data mining application.

Step 2.2: Data Preprocessing

Study the quality of the data to pave the way for further analysis and to determine the kind of mining operation that will be possible and worth performing.

Step 2.3: Data Transformation

Transform the data into an analytical model. Model the data to suit the intended analysis and the data formats required by the data mining algorithms, many of which have particular requirements. Presentation of a sound analytical data model of the data to the mining algorithms is critical to success.

Step 3: Data Mining

Mine the data you transformed in Step 2.3. This is the heart of the matter, and, apart from selecting the appropriate combination of data mining algorithms, it is quick and automated.

Step 4: Analysis of Results

Interpret and evaluate the output from Step 3. The analysis approach you use will vary according to the data mining operation, but typically it will involve some visualization technique.

Step 5: Assimilation of Knowledge

Incorporate the business insights gained from Step 4 into the organization's business and information systems.

For our discussion, let us define the roles of the participants in the data mining steps:

Business analyst   Thoroughly understands the application domain, interprets the objectives, and translates them into business requirements that will serve to define the data and mining algorithms to be used.

Data analyst   Thoroughly understands data analysis techniques and typically has a strong statistical background. Has the expertise and ability to transform business requirements into data mining operations and to select the corresponding data mining technique for each operation.

Data management specialist

> Is skilled in data management techniques and collects the data from operational systems, external databases, or data warehouses.

In the rest of this chapter we explore the five data mining process steps in detail. Our discussion is built around a real data mining application in the area of customer vulnerability analysis (CVA), the development of customer *vulnerability models* that help predict consumer loyalty levels to a particular product or class of products.

Such models are important to packaged goods companies, for example, who aim to secure or increase market share for their new or existing products. Predictions from the vulnerability models help these companies in planning marketing strategies for the launch or promotion of their products. Marketing strategies include in-store promotions, direct mail campaigns, and advertising of discount coupons.

The Process in Detail

In this section we explore each of the steps, identifying for each a set of prerequisites, the input and output, and the typical tasks to be carried out.

Business Objectives Determination

This step in the data mining process has a lot in common with the initial step of any significant project undertaking. The minimum requirements are a perceived business problem or opportunity and some level of executive sponsorship. The first requirement ensures that there is a real, critical business issue that is worth solving, and the second guarantees that there is the political will to do something about it when the project delivers a proposed solution.

This first step can become problematic if it is not tackled properly. Frequently, without even thinking about the objectives, you hear people saying: "Here is the data, please mine it." But, how do you know whether a data mining solution is really needed? The only way to find out is to properly define the business objectives. Ill-defined projects are not likely to succeed or result in added value.

Developing an understanding and careful definition of the business needs is not a straightforward task in general. It requires the collaboration of the business analyst with domain knowledge and the data analyst who can begin to translate the objectives into a data mining application.

This step in the process is also the time at which to start setting expectations. Nothing kills an otherwise successful project as quickly as overstated expectations of what could be delivered. Managing expectations will help to avoid any misunderstandings that may arise as the process evolves, and, especially, as the final results begin to emerge.

Let us take an example. Data mining projects to improve the response rates to mailing campaigns typically have objectives to increase the rate from the current 1% to 2%-2.5%. So, although individual campaigns may vary, in general, expectations of returns that are significantly above these levels will probably not be possible and will most likely doom the project to failure.

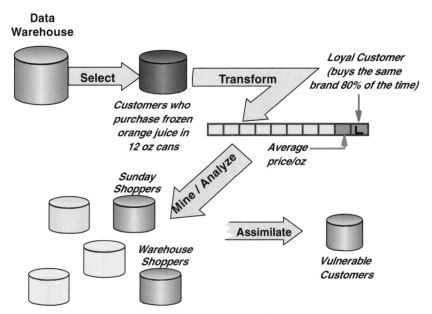

Figure 13. *The Data Mining Process: CVA Example*

A first-cut cost-benefit analysis is also an essential undertaking during this step. The effort to be expended must be commensurate with the potential benefits. See "The Business Case" on page 132 for more details on this topic.

As a by-product of this initial step, the team of business analyst and data analyst may also begin to make some preliminary identification of the data mining algorithms and databases that are relevant to the business objectives.

With regard to the CVA project, the business objective was to develop a marketing strategy to maintain the current market share for a particular brand and size (12-oz. can) of frozen orange juice in the Midwestern U.S. during the months of November, December, and January. The company would use a combination of marketing strategies, one of which was to be a direct mail campaign aimed at those customers who were perceived to be vulnerable. The key question was, Which households should be included in the direct mail campaign for the effort to be successful? Figure 13 on page 46 illustrates the overall strategy of the data mining project team. The team used syndicated data as a basis to build models of the typical buying patterns of both vulnerable and loyal customers. Once these behavioral rules were visible and understood, the team segmented the customer database into homogeneous groups for targeting by different marketing campaigns.

Data Preparation

Data preparation is the most resource-consuming step in the process, typically requiring up to 60% of the effort of the entire project. This step comprises three phases:

1. Data selection (identification and extraction of data)
2. Data preprocessing (data sampling and quality testing)
3. Data transformation (data conversion into an analytical model)

Data Selection

The goal of data selection is to identify the available data sources and extract the data that is needed for preliminary analysis in preparation for further mining.

Clearly, the data selection will vary with the business objectives, which in turn are determined by the type of application to be used.

Along with each of the selected variables, associated semantic information (metadata) is needed to understand what each of the variables means. The metadata must include not only solid business definitions of the data but also clear descriptions of data types, potential values, original source system, data formats, and other characteristics. There are three major types of variables:

Categorical The possible values are finite and differ in kind. There are two subtypes: nominal and ordinal. Nominal variables name the kind of object to which they refer, but there is no order among the possible values, for example, marital status (single, married, divorced, unknown), gender (male, female), and level of education (university, college, high school). Ordinal variables have an order among the possible values, for example, customer credit rating (good, regular, poor).

Quantitative There is a measurable difference between the possible values. There are two subtypes: continuous (values are real numbers) and discrete (values are integers). Examples of continuous variables are income, average number of purchases, and revenue. Examples of discrete variables are number of employees and time of year (month, season, quarter).

The variables selected for data mining are called *active variables* in the sense that they are actively used to distinguish segments, make predictions, or perform some other data mining operation. In addition, some data mining algorithms allow for the inclusion of supplementary variables. These fields are not used directly in the data mining analysis but are useful in helping to visualize and explain the results.

When you select data, another important consideration is the expected shelf life of the data, that is, the extent to which ongoing changes in external circumstances may limit the effectiveness of the mining. For example, because a percentage of customers will change their jobs every year, any analysis where job type is a factor has to be re-examined periodically. Equally, demographic and lifestyle data tend to have short life expectancies.

At this stage the data analyst has already begun to focus on the data mining algorithms that will best match the business application. This is an important aspect to keep in mind as the other phases of the data preparation step evolve because it will guide the development of the analytical data model and the fine-tuning of the data input. The other major player to emerge at this time is the data management specialist, who will be responsible for collecting and integrating the data into the informational environment.

Looking again at the CVA project, the data selection was done from a syndicated database of some 15,000 consumers whose supermarket purchases had been tracked for three years. From this database, only those consumers who had purchased orange juice more than 25 times in the last three years were selected. The list of items purchased in each supermarket visit was called a basket, and 14 variables were used to describe each basket. These variables included such items as household ID, date of purchase, basket contents, basket value, product quantity, and promotion ID (whether the item was bought at full price, or through some promotion such as coupons).

Data Preprocessing

The aim of data preprocessing is to ensure the quality of the selected data. Clean and well-understood data is a clear prerequisite for successful data mining, just as it is with other quantitative analysis. In addition, by getting better acquainted with the data at hand, you are more likely to know where to look for the real knowledge during the mining stage.

Without a doubt, data preprocessing is the most problematic phase in the data preparation step, principally because most operational data has never been captured or modeled for data mining purposes. Except for cases such as Point of Sale (POS) or other electronically captured data, the selected data is typically collected from numerous, inconsistent, poorly documented operational systems. Even where the data is augmented with external data, trying to match internal and external records can be a major challenge. In any event, although purchased databases often offers up to 400 variables, these are usually very sparsely filled in and can be out of date. The result is that poor data quality and poor data integrity are major issues in almost all data mining projects.

Not surprisingly, then, the data preprocessing phase begins with a general review of the structure of the data and some measuring of its quality. Although the approaches vary, they usually involve a combination of statistical methods and data visualization techniques. Representative sampling of the selected data is a useful technique as large data volumes would otherwise make the review process very time consuming.

For categorical variables, frequency distributions of the values are a useful way of better understanding the data content. Simple graphical tools such as histograms and pie charts can quickly plot the contribution made by each value for the categorical variable and therefore help to identify distribution skews and invalid or missing values.

When dealing with quantitative variables, the data analyst is interested in such measures as maxima and minima, mean (average), mode (most frequently occurring value), median (midpoint value), and several statistical measures of central tendency, that is, the tendency for values to cluster around the mean. When combined, these measures offer a powerful way of determining the presence of invalid and skewed data. For example, maxima and minima analyses quickly show up spurious data values, and the various statistical distribution parameters give useful clues about the level of noise in the data.

Other graphical tools are scatterplots and boxplots. Scatterplots are simple two-dimensional pictures that represent the relationship between two or more continuous variables. Figure 14 is a simple example where the income of a small population of professionals is mapped against their age. The general trend is clear from the plot—income tends to rise with age. However, the objective is to draw a line through the observations, which, in turn, will allow us to predict the income of any professional, given just their age. This simple scatterplot could be augmented by incorporating a third dimension, say, gender. The points on the original scatterplot could be replaced with one type for males and another for females.

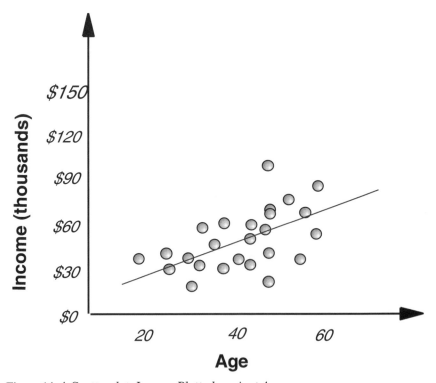

Figure 14. *A Scatterplot: Income Plotted against Age*

Boxplot diagrams can be very useful for comparing the center (average) or spread (deviation) of two or more variables. Figure 15 on page 51 illustrates a boxplot where salary for a sample of men and women is plotted. The rectangles are called the boxes, and the two vertical lines are called the whiskers. Just by observing the size and position of the boxes, we can quickly get a feeling for how the data points are distributed. In this case we can draw the conclusions that men's incomes are greater and more widely spread than women's and that both incomes are skewed to the higher end.

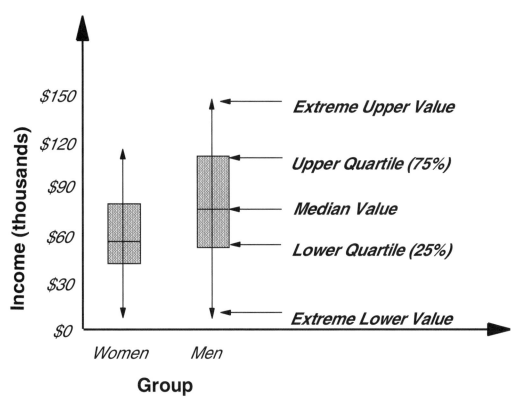

Figure 15. A Boxplot: Income Distribution for Men and Women

Although scatterplots and boxplots are simple devices, they quickly and effectively allow the data analyst to summarize the structure and quality of the data at hand.

During data preprocessing, two of the most common issues are noisy data and missing values.

Noisy Data. With noisy data, one or more variables have values that are significantly out of line with what is expected for those variables. The observations in which these noisy values occur are called outliers. Outliers can indicate good news or bad news—good news in the sense that they represent precisely the opportunities for which we are looking; bad news in that they may well be no more than invalid data.

Different kinds of outliers must be treated in different ways. One kind of outlier may be the result of a human error, for example, a person's age is recorded as 650, or an income is negative. Clearly, these values have to be either corrected (if a valid value or reasonable substitute can be found) or dropped from the analysis. In addition, data checking constraints and/or operational procedures must be reviewed if the source of the data is in-house. If a data warehouse is in use, this checking may be performed more simply when data is loaded into the informational environment.

Another kind of outlier is created when changes in operational systems have not yet been reflected in the data mining environment. For example, new product codes introduced in operational systems show up initially as outliers. Clearly in this case the only action required is to update the metadata.

Skewed distributions often indicate outliers. For example, a histogram may show that most of the people in a target group have low incomes and only a few are high earners. It may be that these outliers are good, in that they represent genuine high earners in this homogeneous group, or it may be that they result from poor data collection; for example, the group may consist mainly of retired people but, inadvertently, include a few working professionals.

In summary, what you do with outliers depends on their nature. You have to distinguish the good outliers from the bad and react appropriately.

Missing Values. Missing values include values that are simply not present in the selected data and those invalid values that we may have deleted during noise detection.

Values may be missing because of human error, because the information was not available at the time of input, or because the data was selected across heterogeneous sources, thus creating mismatches. To deal with missing values, data analysts use different techniques, none of which is ideal.

One technique is simply to eliminate the observations that have missing values. This is easily done but has the obvious drawback of losing valuable data. Although this data loss may be less of a problem in situations where data volumes are large, it certainly will affect results in mining smaller volumes or where fraud or quality control is the objective. In these circumstances we may well be throwing away the very observations for which we are looking. Indeed, the fact that the value is missing may well be a clue to the source of the fraud or quality problem.

If there are a significant number of observations with missing values for the same variable, it may be an option to drop the variable from the analysis. This again has serious consequences because, unknown to the analyst, the variable may have been a key contributor to the solution.

The decision to eliminate data observations and/or variables is never an easy one, nor can the consequences be easily foreseen. Luckily, there are several ways around the problem of missing values. One approach is to replace the missing value with its most likely value. For quantitative variables, this most likely value could be the mean or mode. For categorical variables, it could be the mode or a newly created value for the variable, called UNKNOWN, for example. A more sophisticated approach for both quantitative and categorical variables is to use a predictive model to predict the most likely value for a variable on the basis of the values of the other variables in the observation. Predictive modeling is discussed in detail in "Predictive Modeling" on page 64.

Despite this stockpile of weapons to combat the problem of missing data, you must remember that all of this averaging and predicting comes at a price. The more guessing you have to do, the further away from the real data the database becomes. This, in turn, can quickly begin to affect the accuracy and validity of the data mining results.

In the CVA project, the team summarized the three-year history of data for each household into a single record by creating 20 new variables, including Primary-Brand (the orange juice brand of which the household bought the most ounces), Purchase-Frequency (the ratio of the number of purchases to the number of days between the first and last supermarket visit), and Ounces-Per-Day (the ratio of the number of ounces of orange juice purchased to the number of days between the first and last supermarket visit).

Finally, the team had to define the concepts of a vulnerable consumer and a loyal consumer. It was decided that any consumer who purchased the same brand of orange juice more than 80% of the time would be considered loyal. All others were labeled vulnerable. The resulting database, called the OJ database, had 1,986 records, and each record was labeled as either loyal or vulnerable.

Data Transformation

During data transformation, the preprocessed data is transformed to produce the analytical data model. The analytical data model is an informational data model, and it represents a consolidated, integrated, and time-dependent restructuring of the data selected and preprocessed from the various operational and external sources. This is a crucial phase as the accuracy and validity of the final result depend vitally on how the data analyst decides to structure and present the input. For example, if a department store wants to analyze customer spending patterns, the analyst must decide whether the analysis is to be done at some overall level, at the department level, or at the level of individual purchased articles. Clearly, the shape of the analytical data model is critical to the kinds of problems that the subsequent data mining can solve.

After the model is built, the data is typically further refined to suit the input format requirements of the particular data mining algorithms to be used. The fine-tuning typically involves data recoding and data format conversion and can be quite time-consuming. The techniques used can range from simple data format conversions to complex statistical data reduction tools. Simple data conversions include the conversion of date variables from standard United States or European format to Julian format or the calculation of a customer age variable based on the date of birth in the operational system database. In addition it is quite common to derive new variables from original input data. For example, a data mining run to determine the suitability of existing customers for a new loan product might require as input the average account balance for the last 3-, 6-, and 12-month periods.

Many customer relationship management (CRM) applications use a data transformation technique called *householding*. Here, an organization consolidates its (typically) dispersed customer records to build a profile of its relationship with a particular household. This consolidated profile includes entries for all of the household members along with details of each of the services and/or products of the organization they use.

From statistics, another popular type of transformation is data reduction. Although a general term that involves many different approaches, the basic objective of data reduction is to reduce the total number of variables for processing by combining several existing variables into one new variable. For example, if a marketing department wants to gauge how attractive prospects can be for a new, premium-level product, it can combine several variables that are correlated, such as income, ZIP code, and level of education, to derive a single variable that represents the attractiveness of the prospect. Reducing the number of input variables produces a smaller and more manageable set for further analysis. However, the approach has several drawbacks. It is not always easy to determine which variables can be combined, and combining variables will clearly cause some loss of information. The final result will be all the more difficult to interpret.

Clearly, data remodeling and refining are not trivial tasks in many cases, which helps explain the amount of time and effort that is typically spent in the data transformation phase of the data preparation step.

Most neural networks can accept only numeric input in the 0.0 to 1.0 or -1.0 to +1.0 range. In these cases, continuous parameter values must be scaled so that all have the same order of magnitude. This input format restriction is required to prevent the algorithm from unduly attributing more importance to those variables that have large input values. For example, if income and number of services are two input variables to develop a predictive model, the magnitude of the income variable may assume undue importance over the number of services variable.

Another technique, called *discretization*, involves converting quantitative variables into categorical variables by dividing the values of the input variable into buckets. For example, a continuous variable such as income could be discretized into a categoric variable such as income range. Incomes in the range $0 to $9,999 could be assigned a range of 1, those in the range $10,000 to $19,999 could be assigned a range of 2, and so on.

One-of-N is another common transformation technique that is useful when the analyst needs to convert a categoric variable to a numeric representation, typically for input to a neural network. For example, the categoric variable, *type of car*, could be transformed into a quantitative variable with a length equal to the number of different possible values for the original variable and having an agreed coding system. For example, values of Ford, Lincoln, and Nissan could be represented by transformed values of 100, 010, and 001, respectively.

Data Mining

At last we come to the step in which the actual data mining takes place. The objective is clearly to apply the selected data mining algorithm or algorithms to the preprocessed data.

For clarity in this discussion, we present the data mining step as a separate step. However, in reality it is almost inseparable from the next step in this process, analysis of results. The two are closely interlinked, and the analyst typically iterates around the two for some time during the data mining process. In fact, this iteration often requires a step back in the process to the data preparation step. Two steps forward, one step back often describes the reality of this part of the data mining process.

Physically, the data mining step amounts to running the algorithms, and it is clearly within the domain of the data analyst, occasionally assisted by the data management specialist if issues of data structure, content, or meaning arise. For input, the data analyst is equipped with the preprocessed data from the previous steps, the corresponding metadata and, most importantly, the insight into the underlying data content from the foregoing analysis.

What happens during the data mining step will vary with the kind of application that is under development. For example, in the case of a database segmentation, one or two runs of the algorithm may be sufficient to clear this step and move into analysis of the results. However, if the analyst is developing a predictive model, there will be a cyclical process where the models are repeatedly trained and retrained on sample data before being tested against the real database. Data mining developments typically involve the use of several algorithms, for example, where a database is first segmented in preparation for developing separate predictive models on the individual segments. The data analyst will select the specific algorithm or algorithms to run on the basis of a set of factors including the nature of the objective (for example, segmentation or predictive model development), ability to handle certain data types, explicability of the output, scalability, and level of familiarity. Each of the algorithms has its own set of advantages and disadvantages and these, along with some typical usage issues, are outlined in "Predictive Modeling" on page 64.

The CVA project team used a rule induction algorithm to characterize the different consumer behaviors typical for both loyal and vulnerable consumers. The advantage of the rule induction approach is the relative ease with which the results can be understood and analyzed. (The team also used another predictive modeling approach, tree induction, by way of comparison). All results were extensively cross-validated using a technique that is sometimes called *10-fold cross validation*. The entire database was divided into 10 equal parts. The models were then trained on only nine-tenths of the database and tested on the remaining one-tenth, which had been held out. This process was repeated until each of the other tenths had also been used for testing.

Finally, to identify groups of consumers with similar purchasing patterns so that they could be more effectively targeted for marketing campaigns, the team used database segmentation to extract homogeneous subpopulations of consumers from the OJ database.

Analysis of Results

Needless to say, analyzing the results of the mining run is one of the most important steps of the whole process. In addition, in spite of improvements in graphical visualization aids, this step can only properly be done by a skilled data analyst working with a business analyst. Occasionally, reference will have to be made back to the executive sponsor for clarification on findings and business objectives.

The analysis of results is inseparable from the data mining step in that the two are typically linked in an interactive process. The exploratory nature of data mining ensures that this is always the case.

The specific activities in this step depend very much on the kind of application that is being developed. Nevertheless, the single question on the minds of the data mining team always remains the same: Have we found something that is interesting, valid, and actionable? Almost always the answer is *no*, in which case the exploratory cycle repeats itself. In this respect, at least, data mining is different from traditional statistical analysis. With statistics, the answer is generally, *yes* or *no: yes*, the hypothesis is correct, or *no*, it is incorrect. If the latter, it is often back to the drawing board for the team. With data mining, if it is done well, the results either suggest the answer or at least point the team in the direction of another avenue of research.

For example, when performing a customer database segmentation, the data analyst and business analyst attempt to label each of the segments to put some business interpretation on each. Each segment should be homogeneous enough to allow for this. However, if there are only a few segments with large concentrations of customer records, the segment cannot be sufficiently differentiated. In this case, changing the variables on which the segmentation is based improves the result; for example, removing the most common variables from the large segments gives a more granular segmentation on a rerun.

When predictive models are being developed, a key objective is to test their accuracy. Occasionally, these models cannot be made to perform consistently with the required level of accuracy. However, many data mining tools provide helpful facilities, such as confusion matrixes (how well the prediction measures against known actual results) and input sensitivity analyses (the relative importance attributed to each of the input variables). Failure to perform satisfactorily usually guides the team toward the unduly influential input or sends it in search of new input variables. One common source of error when building a predictive model is the selection of overly predictive variables. In the worst case scenario, the analyst may inadvertently select a variable that is recorded only when the event that he or she is trying to predict occurs. Take, for example, a policy cancellation date as input to a predictive model for customer attrition. The model will perform with 100% accuracy, which should be a signal to the team to recheck the input. A good rule of thumb is that if it sounds too good to be true, it probably is.

Another difficulty in predictive modeling is that of overtraining, where the model predicts well on the training data but performs poorly on the real test data. The problem is caused by overexposure to the training data—the model learns the detailed patterns of that data but cannot generalize well when confronted with new observations from the test data set.

Developing association rules also poses special considerations. For example, if confidence levels are set too low, the algorithm will tend to pick up more rules. However, many of the rules will be inactionable or will reflect no more than one-off instances. Equally, if the confidence levels are set too high, only the major rules will be discovered, in which case many of them already will be well known and therefore not actionable. Clearly, this is one area where careful tuning and iteration are needed to derive useful information.

The CVA project produced several interesting results. First, the rule induction algorithm offered an insight into the typical purchasing behavior of both loyal and vulnerable consumers (see Figure 16).

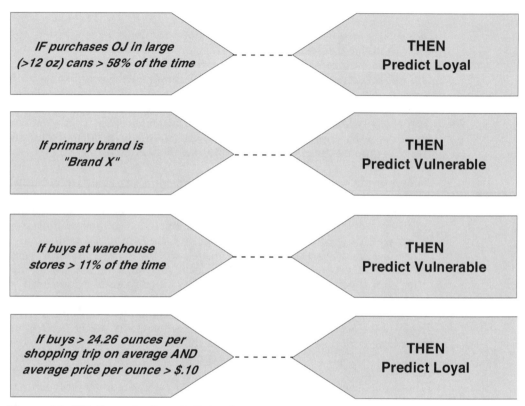

Figure 16. CVA Example: Sample Rules Output

The database segmentation yielded equally interesting results. Five segments were produced, and of these, two were selected for further analysis because of their ease of interpretation. One was a largely loyal group that consisted of heavy orange juice consumers who paid full price for orange juice and made their purchases in food stores, mostly on Sundays. The second segment was largely vulnerable and consisted of heavy orange juice consumers who bought in bulk, paid mostly full price for the orange juice, and purchased it in warehouse stores.

Assimilation of Knowledge

This step closes the loop, which was opened when we set the business objectives at the beginning of the process. The objective now is to put into action the commitments made in that opening step, according to the (presumably) new, valid, and actionable information from the previous process steps.

This step has two main challenges: to present the new findings in a convincing, business-oriented way, and to formulate ways in which the new information can be best exploited.

Clearly, this step is within the domain of the business analyst and is focused on the executive sponsor. The experienced business analyst will be able to formulate the findings in a way that relates directly to the business objectives that were set for the project at the outset. In addition, a data analyst with extensive domain and/or industry knowledge can be a great asset at this stage. Again, the specific business actions to be taken depend on the kind of application being developed and the executive commitments in the opening step. For example, database segmentation is most often done as a forerunner to launching targeted marketing campaigns at the newly identified segments. A new predictive model to improve customer retention could well necessitate several actions such as direct mailings to identified customers and introduction of discounts. A newly discovered set of association rules could spark the development of a marketing campaign to cross-sell new or existing services to existing customers or to prompt the redesign of a shop floor layout to better leverage the revealed shopper preferences.

In addition to the business initiatives, there are several technical issues to consider. At a minimum, the new information may manifest itself as new data mining applications or modifications to be integrated into the existing technical infrastructure. Integration could involve the inclusion of new predictive models and association rules in existing application code, expert system shells, or database procedures. In addition, operational and informational system databases may be enhanced with new data structures. In any event, the experiences during the data preparation step will doubtless put a focus on data integrity in the upstream operational systems. This focus will create a demand for improved data quality and documentation in these systems, and improved manual procedures to prevent error or fraud.

Ultimately, the biggest benefit from the project may well be a recognition of, or a renewed focus on, the importance of the corporate data asset and the power of data-driven solutions. This in turn can engender a culture within the organization that can promote larger, longer-term, data-oriented initiatives such as data warehousing and data marting.

4

Face to Face with the Algorithms

*A computer with as many vacuum tubes as a
man has neurons in his head would require
the Pentagon to house it, Niagara's power to
run it, and Niagara's waters to cool it.*
(Warren S. McCulloch, 1956)

This chapter is for the technically curious who want to know a little
more about the data mining algorithms behind the many applications
we review in Chapter 3, "The Data Mining Process," on page 41. The
chapter is not an exhaustive compilation of all approaches to data
mining; rather we present a general review of the most common data
mining operations and techniques.

From Application to Algorithm

To the newcomer, the plethora of different approaches initially can be
quite confusing, and the situation is not helped by the inconsistent

terminology used among data mining practitioners themselves. Although no single set of terms enjoys universal approval, we offer a frame of reference in Figure 17. You can use the figure as a starting point as well as a graphical table of contents for the rest of this chapter.

	Market Management		Risk Management		Fraud Management
Applications	✓ Target marketing ✓ Customer relationship management ✓ Market basket analysis ✓ Cross selling ✓ Market segmentation		✓ Forecasting ✓ Customer retention ✓ Improved underwriting ✓ Quality control ✓ Competitive analysis		✓ Fraud detection
Operations	Predictive Modeling	Database Segmentation	Link Analysis		Deviation Detection
Techniques	✓ Classification ✓ Value prediction	✓ Demographic clustering ✓ Neural clustering	✓ Associations discovery ✓ Sequential pattern discovery ✓ Similar time sequence discovery		✓ Visualization ✓ Statistics

Figure 17. *Data Mining Applications and Their Supporting Operations and Techniques*

Business Applications

The applications listed in Figure 17 represent typical business applications where data mining is used today (see Chapter 2, "Down to Business," on page 25).

Data Mining Operations

Predictive modeling, database segmentation, link analysis, and deviation detection are the four major operations for implementing any of the business applications. We deliberately do not show a fixed, one-to-one link between the business applications and data mining operations layers, to avoid the suggestion that only certain operations are appropriate for certain applications and vice versa. (On the contrary, really breakthrough results can sometimes come from the use of non-intuitive approaches to problems.) Nevertheless, certain well-established links between the applications and the corresponding operations do exist. For example, modern target marketing strategies are almost always implemented by means of the database segmentation operation. However, fraud detection could be implemented by any of the four operations, depending on the nature of the problem and input data. Furthermore, the operations are not mutually exclusive. For example, a common approach to customer retention is to segment the database first and then apply predictive modeling to the resultant, more homogeneous segments.

Typically the data analyst, perhaps in conjunction with the business analyst, selects the data mining operations to use.

Data Mining Techniques

Techniques are specific implementations of the algorithms that are used to carry out the data mining operations. Each cell in Figure 17 on page 62 should be seen more as a family of algorithms, all of which have the same basic goal. Although the support relationship between data mining operations and techniques is much stronger than that between business applications and data mining operations, use the figure as a guideline only. There can be exceptions. For example, the link analysis operation depends critically on the associations discovery technique, but an interesting deviation is as likely to be detected by an unusually small segment containing only a few records as it is by the use of visualization or statistical techniques.

Not all algorithms to implement a particular data mining operation are equal, and each has its own strengths and weaknesses. A particular vendor will sometimes offer a choice of algorithms to implement a technique. The offering is often based on the suitability for certain input date types, transparency of the mining output, tolerance of missing variable values, level of accuracy possible, and, increasingly, ability to handle large volumes of data. A typical example here is the algorithm for building a classification model. Two general approaches are used: decision trees and neural networks. Decision trees have the advantage of being amenable to postclassification analysis (ideal for credit rating assessments) but are prone to biases in the data. Neural networks are less exposed to noisy data but are not as open to intuitive analysis as decision trees.

Bear in mind that new research is always pushing the bound of possibility, and new and hybrid algorithms are always in the making. This is a fast-evolving area.

The key message is this: There is rarely one, fool-proof technique for any given operation or application, and the success of the data mining exercise relies critically on the experience and intuition of the data analyst.

Data Mining Operations

In this section we discuss in detail the operations associated with data mining.

Predictive Modeling

Predictive modeling is akin to the human learning experience, where we use observations to form a model of the essential, underlying characteristics of some phenomenon. For example, in its early years, a young child observes several different examples of dogs and can then later in life use the essential characteristics of dogs to accurately identify (classify) new animals as dogs. This predictive ability is critical in that it helps us to make sound generalizations about the world around us and to fit new information into a general framework.

In data mining, we use a predictive model to analyze an existing database to determine some essential characteristics about the data. Of course, the data must include complete, valid observations from which the model can learn how to make accurate predictions. The model must be told the correct answer to some already solved cases before it can start to make up its own mind about new observations. When an algorithm works in this way, the approach is called *supervised learning*. Physically, the model can be a set of IF THEN rules in some proprietary format, a block of SQL, or a segment of C source code.

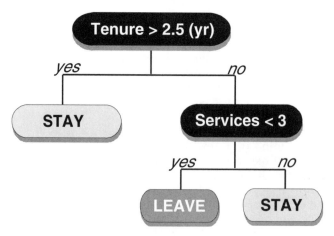

Figure 18. *Predictive Modeling*

Figure 18 illustrates the predictive modeling approach. Here a service company, for example, an insurance company, is interested in understanding the increasing rates of customer attrition. A predictive model has determined that only two variables are of interest—the length of time the client has been with the company (Tenure) and the number of the company's services that the client uses (Services). The decision tree presents the analysis in an intuitive way. Clearly, those customers who have been with the company less than two and one-half years and use only one or two services are the most likely to leave.

Models are developed in two phases: training and testing. Training refers to building a new model by using historical data, and testing refers to trying out the model on new, previously unseen data to determine its accuracy and physical performance characteristics. Training is typically done on a large proportion of the total data available, whereas testing is done on some small percentage of the data that has been held out exclusively for this purpose.

The predictive modeling approach has broad applicability across many industries. Typical business applications that it supports are customer retention management, credit approval, cross selling, and target marketing.

There are two specializations of predictive modeling: *classification* and *value prediction*. Although both have the same basic objective—to make an educated guess about some variable of interest—they can be distinguished by the nature of the variable being predicted.

With classification, a predictive model is used to establish a specific class for each record in a database. The class must be one from a finite set of possible, predetermined class values. The insurance example in Figure 18 on page 64 is a case in point. The variable of interest is the class of customer, and it has two possible values: STAY and LEAVE.

With value prediction, a predictive model is used to estimate a continuous numeric value that is associated with a database record. For example, a car retailer may want to predict the lifetime value of a new customer. A mining run on the historical data of present long-standing clients, including some agreed-upon measure of their financial worth to date, produces a model that can estimate the likely lifetime value of new customers. Apart from the financial worth, some of the other variables to be considered in building the model are the age of customer, income, history of car upgrades, number of people in family, social connections, education level, current profession, (previous) number of years as a customer, and use of financing and service facilities.

A specialization of value prediction is *scoring*, where the variable to be predicted is a probability or propensity. Probability and propensity are similar in that they are both indicators of likelihood. Both use an ordinal scale, that is, the higher the number, the more likely it is that the predicted event will occur. Typical applications are the prediction of the likelihood of fraud for a credit card or the probability that a customer will respond to a promotional mailing.

Database Segmentation

The goal of database segmentation is to partition a database into segments of similar records, that is, records that share a number of properties and so are considered to be homogeneous. (In some literature the words *segmentation* and *clustering* are used interchangeably. Here, we use *segmentation* to describe the data mining operation, and *segments* or *clusters* to describe the resulting groups of data records. By definition, the records in different segments are different in some way. The segments should have high internal (within segment) homogeneity and high external (between segment) heterogeneity. Homogeneity means that records in a segment are in close proximity to each other, where proximity is expressed by a measure dependent on the distance of records from the center of the segment. Heterogeneity means that records in different segments are not similar to each other according to a measure of similarity.

Database segmentation is typically done to discover homogeneous sub-populations in a customer database to improve the accuracy of the profiles. A subpopulation, which might be "wealthy, older, males" or "urban, professional females," can be targeted for specialized treatment. Equally, as databases grow and are populated with diverse types of data, it is often necessary to partition them into collections of related records to obtain a summary of each database or before performing a data mining operation such as predictive modeling.

Figure 19 on page 67 shows a scatterplot of income and age from a sample population. The population has been segmented into clusters (indicated by the circles) which represent significant subpopulations within the database. For example, one cluster might be labeled "young, well-educated professionals," and another, "older, highly paid managers."

The grid lines and shaded sectors on the plot illustrate the comparative inefficiency of the traditional, slice-and-dice approach to the problem of database segmentation. The overlaid areas both do not account for the truly homogeneous clusters because they either miss many of the cluster members or take in extraneous ones—which will skew the results.

In contrast, the segmentation algorithm can segment a database without any prompting from the user about the type of segments or even the number of segments it is expected to find in the database. Thus, any element of human bias or intuition is removed, and the true discovery nature of the mining can be leveraged. When an algorithm works in this way, the approach is called *unsupervised learning*.

Database segmentation can be accomplished by using either demographic or neural clustering methods. The methods are distinguished by:

❑ The data types of the input attributes that are allowed

❑ The way in which they calculate the distance between records (that is, the measure of similarity or difference between the records, which is the essence of the segmentation operation)

❑ The way in which they organize the resulting segments for analysis

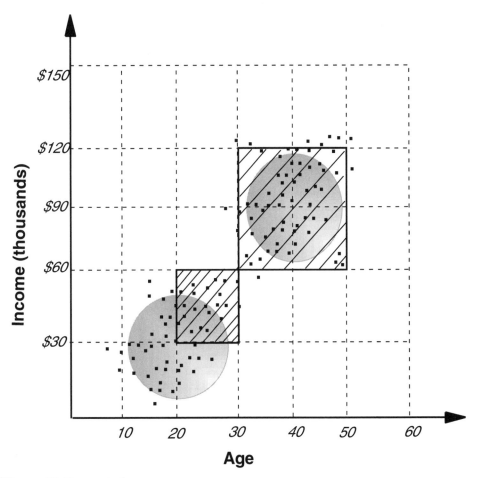

Figure 19. Segmentation

Demographic clustering methods operate primarily on records with categoric variables. They use a distance measurement technique based on the voting principle called *Condorset*, and the resulting segments are not prearranged on output in any particular hierarchy.

Neural clustering methods are built on neural networks, typically using Kohonen feature maps. Neural networks accept only numeric inputs, but categorical inputs are possible by first transforming them into quantitative variables. The distance measurement technique is based on Euclidean distance, and the resulting segments are arranged in a hierarchy where the most similar segments are placed closest together.

Segmentation differs from other data mining techniques in that its objective is generally far less precise than the objectives of predictive modeling or link analysis. As a result, segmentation algorithms are sensitive to redundant and irrelevant features. This sensitivity can be alleviated by directing the segmentation algorithm to ignore a subset of the attributes that describe each instance or by assigning a weight factor to each variable. (Increasing the weight of a variable increases the likelihood that the algorithm will segment according to that variable.) The importance of variables, especially numeric-valued variables, can be established by using univariate and bivariate statistical methods.

Segmentation supports such business applications as customer profiling or target marketing, cross selling, and customer retention. Clearly, this operation has broad, cross-industry applicability.

Link Analysis

In contrast to the predictive modeling and database segmentation operations, which aim to characterize the contents of the database as a whole, the link analysis operation seeks to establish links between the individual records, or sets of records, in the database. These relationships are often called *associations*. A classic application of this operation is associations discovery, that is, discovering the associations between the products or services that customers tend to purchase together or in a sequence over time. Other examples of business applications that link analysis supports are cross selling, target marketing, and stock price movement.

There are three specializations of link analysis: associations discovery, sequential pattern discovery, and similar time sequence discovery.

The differences among the three are best illustrated by some examples. If we define a transaction as a set of goods purchased in one visit to a shop, associations discovery can be used to analyze the goods purchased within the transaction to reveal hidden affinities among the products, that is, which products tend to sell well together. This type of analysis is called *market basket analysis (MBA)* or *product affinity analysis.*

Sequential pattern discovery is used to identify associations across related purchase transactions over time that reveal information about the sequence in which consumers purchase goods and services. It aims to understand long-term customer buying behavior and thus leverage this new information through more timely promotions.

Similar time sequence discovery, the discovery of links between two sets of data that are time-dependent, is based on the degree of similarity between the patterns that both time series demonstrate. Retailers would use this approach when they want to see whether a product with a particular pattern of sales over time matches the sales curve of other products, even if the pattern match is lagging some time behind. Figure 20 shows an example of three apparently unrelated patterns that could represent sales histories or even stock movements over time. At first glance the graphs appear not to be related in any significant way. However, on closer examination, definite patterns can be identified, which, when translated into business terms, can be exploited for commercial gain.

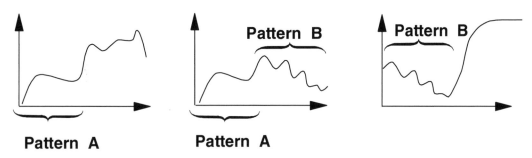

Figure 20. Pattern Matching

Deviation Detection

Deviation detection is a new operation whose importance is just being recognized. The first data mining algorithms automating the operation are only now beginning to appear. Interestingly, it is often the source of true discovery because outliers express deviation from some previously known expectation and norm.

Today, analysts perform deviation detection, using statistics and visualization techniques or as a by-product of data mining. Linear regression facilitates the identification of outliers in data. Modern visualization techniques available on high-powered computers enable the summarization and graphical representations that make deviations easy to detect. Some data mining operations will tend to show up deviations as a useful by-product of their main analysis. For example, if a database segmentation produces a cluster with only a few records, that cluster is quite likely to hold outliers and therefore requires further investigation.

The business applications that deviation detection supports include fraud detection in the use of credit cards, insurance claims, and telephone cards; quality control; and defects tracing.

Data Mining Techniques

At this point it may be useful to refer to Figure 17 on page 62 to understand the structure of this section. In fact, you may prefer not to read this section from end to end but to use it instead as a reference source.

Predictive Modeling: Classification

We discuss here two data mining specializations for classification: tree induction and neural induction. Both are based on supervised learning, the process of automatically creating a classification model from a set of records (examples) called a *training set*. The records in the training set must belong to a small set of classes that the analyst has predefined. The induced model consists of patterns, essentially generalizations over the records, that are useful for distinguishing the classes. Once a model is induced, it can be used to automatically predict the class of other unclassified records. Supervised induction techniques can be either neural or symbolic. Neural techniques, such as back propagation, represent the model as an architecture of nodes and weighted links. Symbolic techniques create models that are represented either as decision trees, or as IF THEN rules.

Supervised induction techniques offer several advantages over statistical-model-creation methods. In particular, the induced patterns can be based on local phenomena, whereas many statistical measures check only for conditions that hold across an entire population with a well-understood distribution. For example, an analyst might want to know whether one attribute is useful for predicting another in a population of 10,000 records. If the attribute is not predictive in general but for a certain range of 100 values is very predictive, a statistical correlation test will almost certainly indicate that the attributes are completely independent because the subset of the data that is predictive is such a small percentage of the entire population.

Tree Induction. A tree induction technique builds a predictive model in the form of a decision tree, often a binary tree as we assume for convenience in this discussion (see Figure 21).

Our example is taken from the customer attrition case where all customers are classified into those likely to stay with the company and those likely to leave (see Figure 18 on page 64). The algorithm starts by identifying the most important variable, that is, the one that it deems to be most influential in determining the classification. In this case, the most important variable is the number of years that the customer has been with the company. The algorithm effectively divides the client database into two parts—those who have been with the company for more than two and one-half years and those who have not. It then assigns the Tenure variable and the associated test condition to the top node in the tree. All records in the training set are then tested against this condition. Those that satisfy the test are sent down the left branch of the node, and those that do not satisfy the test are sent down the right branch. The algorithm then decides on the next important variable, in this case, the Services variable, that is, the number of services the customer uses, and the cycle repeats itself until the tree is fully constructed.

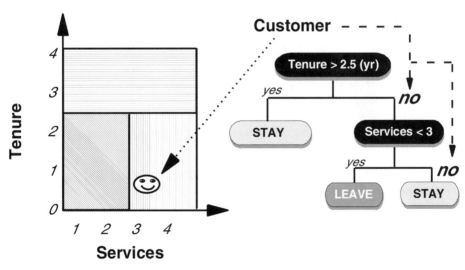

Figure 21. A Binary Decision Tree

The algorithm decides on the test condition automatically. If the associated variable is categorical, the split is between groups of values. Continuous data types are split at some derived threshold value. The decision points are called *nodes,* and the end points where the data observations are collected are called *leaves.*

The tree induction technique is very efficient in terms of processing time and provides a very intuitive method of analyzing the results, as our example shows. This intuitiveness, especially when contrasted with the less accessible output from neural induction, discussed next, explains why decision trees are currently attracting much attention. In fact, tree induction is a must in such applications as loan approval, where the decision to approve or reject the loan must be rationalized.

It is possible to control various aspects of the decision tree algorithm during the training phase. For example, in an effort to control the unwieldy growth of the tree, an analyst can specify the maximum number of levels permissible on the tree or that each leaf must contain a minimum of 10% of the entire training set.

Decision trees have several drawbacks, however. Some decision tree classifiers are not foolproof and may not work with some types of data. Other decision tree classifiers have problems processing sets of continuous data, such as income or prices. Such data and its values may first have to be grouped into ranges or buckets. Whether this grouping is done manually or automatically by the data mining software, the selection of the buckets can unwittingly hide patterns that we would otherwise have discovered from the start.

In addition, decision trees are limited to problems that can be solved by dividing the solution space into successively smaller rectangles. Figure 21 on page 71 illustrates this point. The space is first divided into those customers who have been with the company for more than two and one-half years and those who have not. Those customers who have been with the company less than two and one-half years are then divided into those who use less than and those who use more than three services.

Current decision tree induction methods are not optimal. During the formation of a decision tree, once the algorithm makes a decision about the basis on which to split the node, that decision is never revised. In our case, once the algorithm had decided that "Tenure > 2.5 years" was the most influential factor, it did not look for any new evidence on which to revise the decision. This loss of revision is due to the absence of backtracking, something for which most neural networks make provision.

Another problem area with decision trees is their handling of missing values. Whether it is categorical data (for which we may decide to recode a missing value to "Unknown" or "No color") or continuous data (for which we may decide to replace a missing value with the average), missing values have a serious impact on the outcome of a decision tree. Imagine what would happen if the value for the Tenure variable were missing in Figure 21 on page 71, and we assigned a mean value of 2.6 years to it!

Decision trees also suffer from fragmentation. When the tree has many layers of nodes, the amount of data that passes through the lower leaves and nodes is so small that accurate learning is difficult. To minimize fragmentation, the analyst can prune or trim back some of the lower leaves and nodes to effectively collapse some of the tree. The result is an improved model where the real patterns rather than the noise are revealed, the tree is built more quickly, and it is simpler to understand.

Finally, in common with all induction methods, decision trees are prone to the problem of *overfitting* (sometimes called *overtraining*), where the model learns the detailed pattern of the specific training data rather than generalizing about the essential nature of the data. In the case of decision trees, the result is that the individual leaves of the trained tree hold only the records that match precisely the corresponding path through the tree. Thus, the model performs very well on the training data but poorly when presented with new data patterns. Pruning can be used to combat overfitting.

Neural Induction. The neural induction technique represents the model as an architecture of nodes and weighted links connecting the nodes and as such is based on neural networks. Neural networks are collections of connected nodes with input, output, and processing at each node. Between the visible input and output layers may be a number of hidden processing layers. Figure 22 on page 74 shows a simple neural network based on the customer attrition example in Figure 18 on page 64.

The circles represent processing units. Each processing unit in one layer is connected to each processing unit in the next layer by a weighted value expressing the strength of the relationship. Weights, shown as lines connecting the processing units, are initially set to small nonzero numbers and are adjusted during training of the network, so that the network output conforms to the desired class values calculated from the data. If the output differs, a correction is calculated and applied to the processing in the nodes in the network. These steps are repeated until a stopping condition is reached such as the percentage of records that were classified correctly on the last pass.

There are literally hundreds of variations of propagation in the neural network literature. However, an implementation called *back propagation* is the most widely used in commercial applications. (The term refers to the manner in which errors are propagated or distributed back from the output layer to the input layer during the development phase of the model.) The two primary virtues of back propagation are that it is simple and easy to understand, and it works for a wide range of problems.

Back propagation is a general-purpose, supervised learning algorithm. Although expensive in terms of computational requirements, a back propagation network with a single hidden layer of processing elements can model any continuous function to any degree of accuracy (given enough processing elements in the hidden layer).

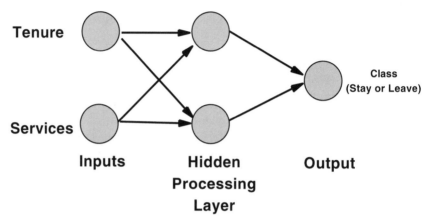

Figure 22. *A Neural Network*

The back propagation algorithm consists of three steps:

1. A set of numeric inputs is presented to the input layer of the network. The input is propagated through the network until it reaches the output units. This forward pass produces the actual or predicted output pattern.

2. Because back propagation is a supervised learning algorithm, the desired output is given as part of the training data. The actual network output is subtracted from the desired output, and an error signal is produced. This error signal is then the basis for the back propagation, which passes the errors back through the neural network by computing the contribution of each hidden processing unit and deriving the corresponding adjustment needed to produce the correct output.

3. The connection weights are then adjusted by means of an error-minimization method called *gradient descent*, and the neural network has then "learned" from an experience.

Because of its inherent provision for revision, the neural induction technique and back propagation are capable of producing optimal solutions. This contrasts to tree induction where backtracking is not present.

Neural induction is more robust than tree induction because of the inherent nature of weighing each data point in the computation of the fitting function. This contrasts to how a recoded missing value can seriously impact the structure of a decision tree.

One drawback of neural induction techniques is that they typically accept only numeric input, so categorical data must be recoded by using, for example, a one-of-N technique.

Neural induction, in common with tree induction, is prone to the problem of overfitting. Luckily, many modern neural networks provide several training parameters that control the rate of learning or the level of error in misclassification. Careful use of these parameters to establish an optimal model can help to alleviate some of the risk of overfitting.

Also, some neural network models fail to converge, that is, they fail to reach a stable level of prediction that matches the acceptance criteria of the analyst. This may occur because there are impurities in the input data or the problem is just too complex for the neural network to solve. In contrast, tree induction does not have this problem.

Some analysts regard neural induction as a type of black-box approach to building a model. The internal rationale that the model uses to make its classifications is not immediately accessible to the analyst. However, two common ways of overcoming some of the difficulty are input sensitivity analysis and confusion matrices. Input sensitivity analysis enables the analyst to determine which input fields were most influential in dictating the actions of the classification model. In fact, in some cases, this information can be as valuable as the model itself.

Confusion matrices offer a measure of the level of effectiveness of the classification model by showing the number of correct and incorrect classifications for each possible value of the variable being classified. Figure 23 on page 76 illustrates a confusion matrix based on the customer attrition example in Figure 18 on page 64.

It is worth spending a little time to understand the structure and value of the matrix. The matrix plots both the correct and incorrect classifications. The correct classifications are in the Will Leave / Left and Will Stay / Stayed cells and the incorrect classifications are in the Will Leave / Stayed and Will Stay / Left cells. Two measures are important when analyzing the effectiveness of the model: coverage and accuracy.

Coverage is the extent to which the model successfully predicted the customers who were going to leave or stay. Obviously we need to know how good the model is at identifying potential leavers. (Of course, the simplest way of guaranteeing total coverage of leavers is to predict that *all* customers will leave, but this is clearly not a viable approach!)

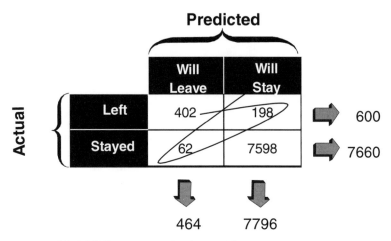

Figure 23. *Model Effectiveness: Confusion Matrix*

In this case the model correctly predicted 402 of the 600 customers who actually left. In other words, the coverage was 67%.

Accuracy is the extent to which the model is correct when it makes a prediction that a customer is going to leave. Here we need to know that we are not incorrectly predicting leavers who are really going to stay. In this case, the model incorrectly predicted that 62 customers were going to leave when they actually stayed. In other words, the error rate was 62 out of 464, or 13%. Thus the accuracy rate is 87%.

Predictive Modeling: Value Prediction

Two traditional techniques used for value prediction are linear regression and nonlinear regression. Linear regression attempts to fit a straight line through a plot of the data, such that the line is the best representation of the average of all observations at that point in the plot (see Figure 14 on page 50).

However, linear regression has some shortcomings. First, the technique works fine if the data is, in fact, linear. Otherwise the analyst has to resort to adding some nonlinear terms to the linear regression equations, often only by trial and error, which is tedious and time-consuming (see Figure 24 on page 77). Second, the outcome of linear regression can be heavily influenced by just a few outliers, so the technique is not robust (see Figure 25 on page 78).

Although nonlinear regression circumvents both shortcomings of linear regression, it is still not flexible enough to handle all possible shapes of the data plot. This is especially true with high numbers of input variables. In such cases the data may be so complex that it is impossible to model it with a single, nonlinear function.

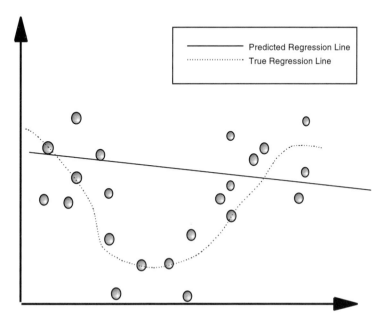

Figure 24. Linear Regression Shortcomings: Nonlinear Data

Radial basis function (RBF) is a new technique for value prediction that demonstrates more robustness and flexibility than traditional regression approaches. RBF works by choosing not just a single nonlinear function, but a weighted sum of a set of nonlinear functions. These weighted functions are the so-called radial-basis functions. The RBFs are each fitted to separate regions in the input space. The regions are chosen such that the output is quite similar within a region, so that the RBF is most likely to fit well to the output. For each selected region, an RBF center is created that predicts the average of the region. Data points that fall between regions are predicted by taking a weighted average of the predictions of all centers, where the weight for a center decays rapidly if the center is very far from that data point.

RBF neural networks are supervised learning models with a single hidden layer of units. They are similar to back propagation neural networks but usually are faster to train because the RBFs used in the units mean that fewer weight adjustments are needed. Also, RBF networks tend to be more resistant to noisy data than back propagation networks.

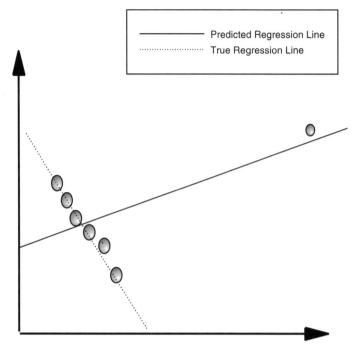

Figure 25. Linear Regression Shortcomings: Outliers

Database Segmentation: Demographic Clustering

The underlying concept of demographic clustering is to build the segments by comparing each record with all segments created by the data mining run. By maximizing the difference between the scores for and against the placement of a record, the algorithm attributes the record to a segment. New segments can be created throughout the run of this process.

The demographic clustering technique relies on a simple voting principle, called *Condorset*, for measuring the distance between input records and thus assigning these records to specific clusters. Pairs of records are compared by the values of the individual fields within them. The number of fields that have similar values determines the degree to which the records are judged to be similar. The number of fields that have dissimilar values determines the degree to which the records are judged to be different. (For noncategorical variables, predetermined tolerances are established within which the variables are considered similar.) When a pair of records has the same value for the same field, the field gets a vote of +1. When a pair of records does not have the same value for a field, the field gets a vote of -1. This mechanism can be thought of as awarding scores for and against the similarity of the two records.

Finally, the overall score is calculated as the sum of scores for and against placing the record in a given cluster. The basic idea is that a record is then assigned to another cluster if the overall score is higher than the overall scores if the record were assigned to any of the other clusters. If the overall scores turn out to be negative, the record is now a candidate for placing it in its own cluster. Of course, there are a number of passes over the set with records, as each record must be reviewed for potential reassignment to a different segment. Clusters and their centers are therefore updated continuously within each pass, until either the maximum number of passes is achieved, or the maximum number of clusters is reached and the cluster centers do not change significantly as measured by a user-determined margin.

Demographic clustering has advantages both in its ability to automatically determine the number of segments to be generated and in the clarity of the resulting partitioning of large data sets. In addition, the technique provides fast and natural ordering of very large databases. Once sufficient large clusters are formed, the decision for placing a next record in a cluster, where a large set of records is involved, is not done by comparing each field value of this record with field values of all records in all clusters. It is done by comparing the field values of this record against the value distributions of each field, where these distributions are calculated per cluster on the basis of the records in each cluster.

In contrast to neural clustering, which is suitable for numerical data only, demographic clustering is particularly suitable for categorical data, especially with a small number of categories. It can also treat noncategorical variables, but in these cases the analyst must establish a set of predetermined tolerances. The algorithm uses these tolerances in determining the similarity or dissimilarity of two variables. Values within the tolerances register a vote in favor of equality; values outside the tolerances register a vote against equality. The measure of similarity is now not just a simple binary value (0,1), but varies from 0 to 1. Zero indicates values far apart, 1 indicates identical values, and 0.5 indicates that the values are separated by exactly the value of the tolerance.

Database Segmentation: Neural Clustering

The neural clustering technique employs a Kohonen feature map neural network. Kohonen feature maps use a process called self-organization to configure the output units into a topological map. In contrast to back propagation which is a supervised learning algorithm, Kohonen feature maps are based on unsupervised learning.

Bigus (1996) describes neural clustering by feature map thus:

A feature map neural network consists of two layers of processing units, an input layer fully connected to a competing output layer. There are no hidden units. When an input pattern is presented to the feature map, the units in the output layer compete with each other for the right to be declared the winner. The winning output unit is typically the unit whose incoming connection weights are the closest to the input pattern (in terms of Euclidean distance). Thus, the input is presented and each output unit computes its closeness or match score to the input pattern. The output that is deemed closest to the input pattern is declared the winner, and so earns the right to have its connection weights adjusted. The connection weights are moved in the direction of the input pattern by a factor determined by a learning rate parameter. This is the basic nature of competitive neural networks.

The Kohonen feature map creates a topological mapping by adjusting not only the winner's weights, but also adjusting the weights of the adjacent output units in close proximity or in the neighborhood of the winner. So not only does the winner get adjusted, but the whole neighborhood of output units gets moved closer to the input pattern. Starting from randomized weight values, the output units slowly align themselves such that when an input pattern is presented, a neighborhood of units responds to the input pattern. As training progresses, the size of the neighborhood radiating out from the winning unit decreases. Initially large numbers of output units will be updated, and later on smaller and smaller numbers are updated until at the end of training only the winning unit is adjusted. Similarly, the learning rate decreases as training progresses, and in some implementations, the learn rate decays with the distance from the winning output unit.

From a data mining perspective, two sets of useful information are available from a trained feature map neural network:

❏ Similar customers, products, or behaviors are automatically clustered together so that marketing messages can be targeted at homogeneous groups.
❏ The information in the connection weights of each cluster defines the typical attributes of an item that falls into that segment. This information lends itself to immediate use for evaluating what the clusters mean.

Link Analysis: Associations Discovery

The purpose of associations discovery is to find items that imply the presence of other items in the same transaction. Consider a database of purchases where each purchase (transaction) consists of several articles (items) bought by a customer. Applying an associations discovery technique against this set of transactions will uncover affinities among the collection of items. These affinities between items are represented by association rules. A rule displays, in a textual format, which items imply the presence of other items. Figure 26 illustrates a rule derived from a shopping basket analysis.

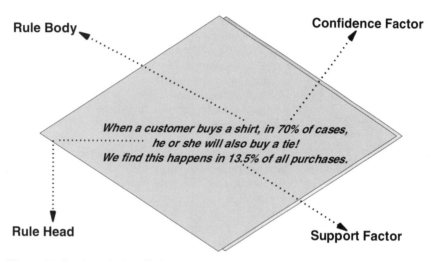

Rule Body

Confidence Factor

When a customer buys a shirt, in 70% of cases, he or she will also buy a tie! We find this happens in 13.5% of all purchases.

Rule Head

Support Factor

Figure 26. *An Association Rule*

Generically, the rule has the form "If X, then Y." *X* is called the rule body, and *Y* is the rule head. Association algorithms are quite efficient at deriving rules. In fact, deriving the rules is not the issue. Rather, the challenge for the analyst is to make a judgment about the validity and importance of the rules. Two parameters are important in this respect: support factor and confidence factor.

The support factor indicates the relative occurrence of the detected association rules within the overall data set of transactions. It is a relative measure as it is determined by dividing the number of transactions supporting the rule by the total number of transactions. A transaction supports the rule "When X then Y" if items X and Y in the rule also occur in the transaction. In the example in Figure 26, the rule is supported by 13.5% of the database records.

The confidence factor of an association rule is the degree to which the rule is true across individual records. It is calculated by dividing the number of transactions supporting the rule by the number of transactions supporting the rule body only. In the example, the confidence factor is 70%.

The associations discovery technique is based on counting occurrences of all possible combinations of items. First, before mining for associations, the transaction IDs are ordered sequentially in the input source. Then the technique starts with counting the occurrences of all single items present in the data set with transactions and creates a one-dimensional column, or vector, where cells hold a count for an item. From then on all cells are ignored where the count is below the support level. Next a two-dimensional array, or matrix, is formed to store counts of occurrences of each item with each other possible item, and again cells are filtered out with a support below the threshold value. When a frequency count is done for a possible third item within the same transaction, a three-dimensional cube occurs, and the process is repeated. So the technique involves reading a data set sequentially from top to bottom each time a new dimension is added and doing simple counts of occurrences.

Clearly, the average number of items per transaction can affect performance. For example, scanning for rules with just one item in the rule body and one item in the rule head takes far less time than scanning for, say, eight items in the body and two items in the head.

The outcome of applying the algorithm against a set of transactions is a list of patterns that state affinities among items, often in a format similar to that in Figure 26 on page 81. For each rule the support and confidence factor are stated. And additional statistics may be supplied such as the *lift* of the association. Lift is best explained by an example: If the support factor for ties in the overall set of transactions is 20% (that is, in 20% of transactions, ties are bought), and the confidence factor for the association between shirts and ties is again 70%, the lift is 3.5, indicating that the expected occurrence of a tie in a transaction is more than threefold if it occurs in a transaction where shirts are bought.

Rules based on high support and confidence factors represent a higher degree of relevance than rules with low support and confidence factors. Note, however, if the support and confidence factors are too high, association rules may not be discovered. If the factors are too low, there will be many possible combinations of product associations, which is not what we seek. The probability of a spurious correlation rises exponentially with the size of the data set. So any large data set is certain to contain some correlations.

Associations discovery enjoys the big advantage of being very simple. The support and confidence factors are the only two parameters that have to be set, and the resulting rules lend themselves to intuitive interpretation.

Additionally, the technique by itself scales well, because it is simply a matter of counting occurrences of all possible combinations of items and involves reading a table sequentially from top to bottom each time a new dimension is added. Thus the technique is particularly suitable for handling a huge number of transactions that may be based on a number of items in the magnitude of tens of thousands is often the case in retail.

One disadvantage of associations discovery is that there is no provision for taking into account the business value of an association. For example, in terms of association rules discovered, the sale of an expensive bottle of white wine accounts for as much as the sale of a carton of milk.

Link Analysis: Sequential Pattern Discovery

The sequential pattern discovery techniques detect patterns between transactions such that the presence of one set of items is followed by another set of items in a database of transactions over a period of time.

For example, given a database of purchases (transactions), transaction date and time or equivalent (transaction ID), and customers (transaction group), each transaction consists of an item set.

❑ Each transaction is identified by its date and time (transaction ID).

❑ Each item is identified by a unique item identifier (item ID).

❑ Each customer is identified by a unique customer identifier (transaction group).

As with associations discovery, the concept of support factor is important in sequential pattern discovery. The actual computation differs from the computation of the support factor for associations, but the definitions are much alike. The support factor indicates the relative occurrence of the detected sequential patterns within the overall data set of transactions. It is a relative measure, determined by dividing the number of customers supporting the sequence by the total number of customers.

Figure 27 on page 84 shows a beverage store owner's database with transaction details.

The data is sorted on customer ID and transaction ID. For instance, customer B. Moore visited the store on three consecutive days. He purchased beer on the first day; wine and cider, the next day; and brandy, the third day.

The customer sequences are organized by transaction (see Figure 28 on page 84).

Each set of parentheses in the sequences indicates a transaction that includes one or more items. For instance, B. Moore bought two items, wine and cider, in his second transaction.

Customer	Transaction Time	Items Bought
B. Adams	June 21, 1994 5:27 pm	Beer
B. Adams	June 22, 1994 10:34 am	Brandy
J. Brown	June 20, 1994 10:13 am	Juice, Coke
J. Brown	June 20, 1994 11:47 am	Beer
J. Brown	June 21, 1994 9:22 am	Wine, Water, Cider
J. Mitchell	June 21, 1994 3:19 pm	Beer, Gin, Cider
B. Moore	June 20, 1994 2:32 pm	Beer
B .Moore	June 21, 1994 6:17 pm	Wine, Cider
B. Moore	June 22, 1994 5:03 pm	Brandy
F. Zappa	June 20, 1994 11:02 am	Brandy

Figure 27. *Sequential Pattern Discovery: Transaction Database*

The technique does a frequency count for each combination of transactions it can produce from the customer sequences and displays those sequential patterns whose relative occurrence is larger than the required minimum support level (see Figure 29 on page 85).

Customer	Customer Sequences
B. Adams	(Beer)(Brandy)
J. Brown	(Juice, Coke)(Beer)(Wine, Water, Cider)
J. Mitchell	(Beer, Gin, Cider)
B. Moore	(Beer)(Wine,Cider)(Brandy)
F. Zappa	(Brandy)

Figure 28. *Sequential Pattern Discovery: Customer Sequence*

Sequential Patterns with Support > 40%	Supporting Customers
(Beer) (Brandy)	B. Adams, B. Moore
(Beer) (Wine, Cider)	J. Brown, B. Moore

Figure 29. *Sequential Pattern Discovery: Support > 40%*

As it turns out, the sequential pattern "beer is bought in a transaction before brandy is bought in a subsequent transaction" occurs for two out of the five customers.

The advantages and disadvantages of associations discovery (see "Link Analysis: Associations Discovery" on page 80) also apply to sequential pattern discovery. There are a few additional points to address, however. First, only one parameter needs to be specified, the support factor. Second, a large number of records is needed to ensure a representative number of transactions per customer. Third, the extra field is required to represent the customer ID; not many companies, particularly retailers have this field stored in the transaction database. Fourth, for the technique to perform well, the data should be sorted beforehand on date and time (transaction ID) and customer identifier (transaction group).

Link Analysis: Similar Time Sequence Discovery

Similar time sequence discovery finds all occurrences or similar occurrences, or finds sequences similar to a given sequence, in a database of time-series data. A time series is a set of values of one variable over a period of time. On the horizontal axis, time is plotted in discrete, constant units, for example, months or days. On the vertical axis, values of the variable are plotted, for example, sales of products or prices of mutual funds or stocks. In both cases, the technique relies on the availability of time sequences.

Let's say a retailer wants to optimize purchasing and storekeeping. He can look at daily or weekly sales of products or product groups and see which product groups had similar sales over a given period or notice whether any group leads or lags behind another product group. In his database, a number of sequences represent sales fluctuations over a period of days or weeks for a number of products. A mining run on this database returns all similar sequences of movements. By interpreting the graphical view of each part of these sequence pairs, the retailer can find groups of products that have similar forecasted seasonal sales for the next year. On the basis of this information, he can optimize purchases and inventory replenishment.

But when are two series considered equal? Because of the inherent randomness of real data, the equality requirement has to be adjusted to achieve a meaningful definition of similarity. Two popular approaches in this area are the introduction of a margin for error and a permissible mismatch gap. The margin for error is the maximum value by which corresponding data in the two series may differ and yet be considered equal. This margin ensures a tolerance for the inherent variability in real time-series data without missing the discovery of essentially similar patterns. The mismatch gap is the number of consecutive time units for which non-matching values are ignored. This gap will ensure that short spikes and troughs in two time series do not disguise an underlying similar pattern.

An advantage of similar time sequence discovery is that movements of several different business items, such as sales volume or price movement of products or stocks, sales per location, and number or dollar amount of claims per medical treatment can be mined without any conditions. Apart from time dependency and that the data are quantitative, no further assumptions are made.

A disadvantage of this technique is that, for the novice user, a number of parameters have to be set and used with care. If you specify a small margin for error, similar time sequence cannot be found although they may be present in the business data. If you specify too large a margin for error, the time series can be considered similar, even if they are not. If you specify too small a mismatch gap, similar time sequences may be hidden. If you specify too high a gap, spurious sequences may be found.

Deviation Detection: Visualization

Visualization techniques are among the most powerful devices for identifying patterns hidden in data. This is not surprising, given that psychologists have long recognized that more than 80% of the information we absorb is received visually. Visualizations are particularly useful for noticing phenomena that hold for a relatively small subset of the data and thus are drowned out by the rest of the data when statistical tests are used (because these tests generally check for more global features).

Importantly, when you use visualization, you need not stipulate a hypothesis—for example, a type of phenomenon you are looking for—in order to notice something unusual or interesting.

There are many ways of visualizing data. For univariate data, that is, one dimension or variable, typically histograms, scatterplots, boxplots, and pie-charts have been used. Graphs and three-dimensional graphical surface plots are useful for low-dimensional data, that is, one, two, or three variables. For higher dimensional data, for example, where results with ten or more variables have to be displayed, these tools are not adequate, prompting the development of new ways to graphically represent multivariate data in an easy-to-understand way. Figure 30 is a three-dimensional scatterplot that shows the probability of fraud for certain characteristics for a customer set, namely, work duration, net worth, debt-ratio, credit limit, and income. The size of the spheres (called glyphs) indicates the probability of fraud, and a color-coding convention (unfortunately not obvious here) indicates current credit limit.

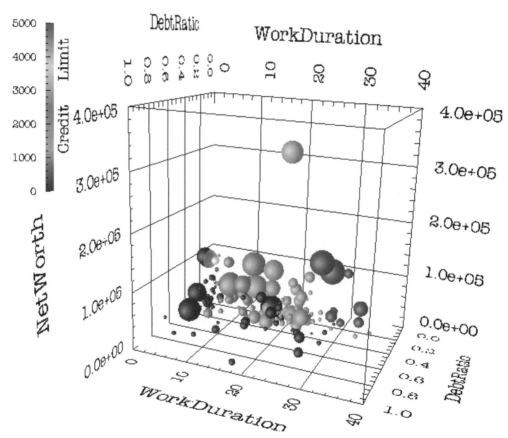

Figure 30. Fraud Probability in Five-Dimensional Space

Visualization techniques also complement other data mining techniques, for example, to graphically show the results of a segmentation or associations discovery run.

Deviation Detection: Statistics

Whereas visualization techniques are useful for actually *detecting* deviations, statistics are used to *measure* their significance. Measuring the significance, or interestingness, of the deviation is clearly critical to knowing what to do with the deviation, once detected. This is true whether statistics are being used in the data preparation phase or the analysis of results phase of the data mining process.

In the data preparation phase, data analysts insist on basic statistical measures as a good way of understanding the nature of the underlying data, including the presence of outliers, which can represent noisy or invalid data. Typical measures include means, medians, frequency counts, and variances. Means and medians are measures of central tendency in a data distribution and can be used to test the significance of suspected deviant values. When the variance of a variable (that is, the extent to which its values differ from its mean) is plotted, it typically takes on the normal bell-shaped curve. The significance of the variance of an individual value of the variable can be tested by using this curve and a measure called standard deviation. For example, given a normal distribution, the probability that a variable will take on a value that is greater than one standard deviation above the mean is only about 17%; that it will be two standard deviations away is only about 3%, and so on.

Statistical measures are also useful in the analysis of results phase. For example, many of the same measures as described above can be used to test out the quality of the segments that have been produced during a database segmentation. Individual segments can be analyzed to understand the level of homogeneity, that is, lack of deviant values, in the segments.

For a general discussion of the challenges in treating deviations in data values, see "Data Preprocessing" on page 49.

5

Evaluating Vendor Solutions

We often overestimate what a new technology
can do in a few months, and underestimate
what it can do in a few years.
(E. Feigenbaum),
P. McCormack,
P. Nii)

In this chapter we present an overview of the general data mining solutions available today—a dangerous undertaking in such a fast-moving environment. However, it is precisely because of this quickly changing environment that it is especially important to have a frame of reference by which to judge the offerings.

We cover three broad categories of solutions—tools, applications, and services—with the intent of advising the prospective data mining teams about what to look for when they go out searching for data mining solutions. We offer general guidelines for evaluating vendor solutions, rather than details or recommendations on any particular vendor offering.

This overview offers only a current snapshot of a fast-evolving area. Doubtless, the choices and decisions will become more complex with the passing of time. However, the basic classifications and differentiators in this chapter will remain valid and a useful homework aid for the prospective data mining team.

Finally, bear in mind that, while good homework is always useful when seeking out a data mining solution, the only way to accurately evaluate vendor solutions is to try them out on a common set of real, in-house business problems.

The Value of Technology

Before launching into the details of evaluating different vendor solutions, it is worth pausing to reflect on the relative importance of the technology offerings to the success of your overall data mining project.

A strong technology is obviously an essential part of the data mining endeavor; the more important aspects of any tool are the data preparation facilities, the selection of data mining algorithms, product scalability and performance, and, critically, the facilities for visualization of results. However, while a strong technology is essential for data mining, it is by no means sufficient for success. Truly successful data mining depends much more on a sharp and sustained business focus and the human element of the endeavor than on any other aspect, including the underlying technology.

Furthermore, as a general rule, the potential ROI from any data mining solution increases exponentially as your solution moves from a data mining tool to an application to a data mining service. In other words, you can expect to get a lot more leverage for your dollar investment from, say, a data mining consultancy engagement than from buying an off-the-shelf product and trying it out yourself.

Data Mining Tools

In recent years there has been a sharp rise in the number of data mining offerings in the marketplace, and this trend will continue for some time. In fact, data mining is currently such an attraction that many vendors of traditional decision support tools are adding data mining capability (or at least, labeling) to their products. The emerging generic title for these tools is *siftware*, because they sift through large amounts of data.

Types of Data Mining Tools

Taking the broadest possible view of the data mining tools available today, they tend to fall into three categories—commercial, public domain, and research prototype. This categorization frequently reflects the academic origins of some of the tools as well as the relative commercial immaturity of this marketplace.

❑ **Commercial**

Mainline products from commercial vendors have structured pricing and support and are often linked to data mining consultancy services. Some examples from this quickly expanding category are:

- Clementine from Integral Solutions Ltd.
- Cross/Z from Cross/Z International Inc.
- DataCrusher from DataMind Corp.
- Database Mining Marksman from HNC Software Inc.
- Intelligent Miner from IBM
- MineSet from Silicon Graphics Inc.
- Data Mining Suite from Information Discovery Inc.
- SAS System (selected procedures and macros) from the SAS Institute Inc.
- Thought from Right Information Systems

❑ **Public domain**

Public domain offerings are typically developed at least in part by academic institutions and are usually available for a modest registration fee. They are effectively free-ware and come largely as is. Some examples are:

- Brute from the University of Washington, Seattle, Washington
- MCL++ from Stanford University, Stanford, California

❑ **Research prototype**

Research prototype offerings typically focus on a narrow area of interest to research teams. However, they may well find their way into commercial products in due course. Examples of these offerings are:

- DB Miner from the Simon Fraser University, British Columbia
- Mining Kernel System from the University of Ulster, Northern Ireland

Of the three categories, clearly the commercial offerings are of most interest to our discussion, and the other categories are not discussed further. That said, not all commercial data mining tools are alike, and it is possible to further categorize them. Two broad categories can be distinguished: generic, single-task tools and generic, multitask tools. Generic, single-task tools, primarily for classification, typically use neural network or decision tree approaches. They cover only the data mining step of the overall data mining process and require extensive pre- and post-processing.

An early tool in this category was the Neural Network Utility introduced by IBM in 1989. 4Thought is another example.

Generic, multitask tools represent an advance on the single-task tools in two ways. First, they support more of the overall data mining process by including, for example, modules for preprocessing and visualization. Second, they typically offer a broad selection of the popular data mining techniques, such as clustering or deviation detection and some statistical processing. The motivation is to solve a wide variety of business problems with a single tool while always having the best tool at hand for any application problem.

Some examples of generic multitask tools are Intelligent Miner, Clementine, and the Data Mining Suite.

What makes a data mining tool worth the investment in money and company time? In this section we present general guidance for the prospective buyer. We assume that the buyer is looking for a commercially available, generic, multitask tool.

Our discussion includes only those aspects of the tools that relate specifically to data mining, for example, selection of mining algorithms, scalability and performance. We do not attempt to address many of the other factors that would normally be part of full commercial evaluation—such as price, vendor support, and available customer references. The two primary evaluation criteria are data mining process support and technical considerations. The data mining process support criterion relates to the extent to which the tool can support the end-to-end data mining process—from data gathering to results visualization. It includes the variety of mining techniques that are supported, for example, the inclusion of several different classification approaches to handle different types of user data and the sensitivity of the algorithms to noisy data. This criterion is always a key consideration but will be most critical in organizations that lack data mining expertise.

The technical considerations criterion covers openness, integration, scalability, overall performance, and extensibility through application development. These are fundamental requirements of any data mining tool, and they are important for all organizations.

Data Mining Process Support

In this section we discuss the requirements for support during the data mining process.

Data Preparation

The data preparation step of the process, involving data selection, data preprocessing, and data transformation, is by far the most labor-intensive one. The tool's facilities in this area should be the focus of much attention during the evaluation process.

By definition, your data mining tools should work against your most valuable corporate data, such as customer histories and EPOS data. This data may well be scattered around the organization in heterogeneous data sources, or, increasingly, it may be held in a relational or multidimensional database. In general, the data mining tool must be able to access as broad a set of sources as possible, including:

❏ Flat files—a common export format for many vendor tools
❏ Hierarchical databases—traditional sources of enterprise data, for example, ADABAS and IMS
❏ Relational databases—including popular sources such as DB2, Informix, Oracle, and Sybase
❏ Multidimensional databases—such as Essbase from Arbor Software—which increasingly important with the OLAP processing and data marts
❏ Other vendor-specific formats—for example, Redbrick, SAS, and SPSS.

After identifying the data sources, look for flexibility in the approach to data selection. For example, you will certainly have to filter the selected data, and, in a distributed data environment, you may have to join several data sources on input to the mining tool.

A wide variety of input data types is also a key requirement. Most tools impose some limitations on the data they can read, but some tools can handle only two or three types, typically numeric and text data. Following is a good starter set of data types:

❏ Categorical
❏ Quantitative

Another important consideration is the number of records or number of attributes that the tool can handle. Some of the commercially available tools have no effective limitations, but many tools, particularly those that are PC-based, are limited in the number of records or attributes they can handle. Some PC tools can work with fewer than 100 attributes while the maximum number of records can be as low as 1,000.

In addition, the way in which users interact with the tool is an important consideration, especially in organizations that are new to data mining. Many tools are (largely) automatic, and there is little or no opportunity to influence their behavior, for example, by setting the maximum number of database segments or the rate at which a neural network should learn. Although this may be a benefit to start with, it can become overly restrictive as user skill levels increase with experience. Other tools are heavily interactive, offering ample opportunity to set parameters, with the associated drawbacks for novices and advantages for expert users. Seek out interactive tools that offer two modes of interaction—expert and novice.

Data Preprocessing and Transformation. Here is the summary of the key functional requirements in the areas of data preprocessing and transformation.

❏ **Sampling**

Sampling of data is the random selection of rows to reduce an input data source to a smaller size while still maintaining a representative content.

❏ **Aggregation**

Aggregation of data is the summarization of input data or the derivation of new data from input data. The output data source always contains one record in one field per Aggregation Expression/New Field Name pair. For relational input sources, SQL column functions such as AVG, COUNT, SUM, and MAX are usually available to the aggregation functions, and some tools even offer compound aggregation expressions, such as AVG(SALARY + COMM), AVG(CHECKING_BALANCE + SAVINGS_BALANCE), and STDDEV(OVERDUE_INTERVAL).

❏ **Symbol mapping**

Symbol mapping, sometimes called *name mapping*, maps data values to more meaningful names or labels or maps strings to numbers. For instance, *Male* and *Female* are more meaningful than the digits 1 and 2, which may be stored in the input database to indicate gender.

❏ **Encoding missing or invalid values**

Encoding replaces data values that are either missing from the input data source or present but did not match a specified value. Some level of support in this area is critical given the generally unclean nature of most initial input data sets and the serious effects of missing and invalid data on many data mining algorithms.

❑ **Text case conversion**

Text case conversion converts lower-case text to upper-case and vice versa. Such conversion may be useful when you require one of the mining algorithms to do an exact string comparison or want visualizations and reports to be consistent with respect to upper-case or lower-case display.

❑ **Discretization**

Discretization is the mapping of a quantitative variable to a range or quantile.

➤ Discretization into ranges

This function maps discrete values to a value that indicates a range by splitting the range of a continuous variable into intervals and then assigning each discrete value to a specific interval.

➤ Discretization into quantiles

This function operates as for ranges, except that the intervals are quantiles.

❑ **Pivoting**

Pivoting is the splitting of a repeating substructure in an input record into separate records, one for each occurrence of the substructure. For example, an input record holding repeating details of insurance claims for a specific policy could be pivoted to provide a separate record for each claim.

Data Mining. By definition, a multitask data mining tool should offer a broad selection of techniques. Not all techniques are equally useful or applicable in each organization. The particular set of techniques that are most appropriate will depend on the application areas that are of most interest. Furthermore, data analysts often use several techniques in an effort to cross-validate mining results. "Face to Face with the Algorithms" on page 61 provides a detailed analysis of the most popular techniques and maps them to common business application problem areas. In addition, for a given data mining technique, data analysts will often want a choice of implementation to give them more flexibility in terms of ease of use, scalability, speed of learning, tolerance of noisy data, and levels of accuracy achievable. A simple rule of thumb could be "The more the merrier."

The number of techniques that vendor tools support varies considerably. A small number of tools support only visualization and one other technique, and an equally small number support all of the techniques described in this book. The most popularly supported techniques in commercial data mining tools today are (in descending order):

❏ Visualization
❏ Classification
❏ Predictive modeling
❏ Segmentation
❏ Associations discovery
❏ Sequential pattern discovery

Analysis of Results and Assimilation of Knowledge. The success of this step in the data mining process is critically dependent on the way in which the tool presents the findings. In "Deviation Detection: Visualization" on page 86 we discuss why visualization itself is an important technique for understanding the information extracted from the data mining runs. Although visualization in data mining serves the same broad purpose it serves in general decision-support processing, it differs in two main respects: the result data sets tend to be large, and some of the results are not data sets per se but sets of rules or predictive models. Both differences influence the approach to the visualization function in the data mining tools. The general approach is for vendors to build some visualization into their products and allow the data or model results to be exported for use with other vendors' visualization tools or custom applications.

Because of the nondata outputs from data mining algorithms, vendors are obliged to provide some sort of specialized display techniques, for example, for viewing and analyzing a decision tree that helps to explain the basis on which the tool has predicted some customer behavior or for viewing the results of a large database segmentation. Although display techniques vary from vendor to vendor, the keynote is the extent to which the tool enables you to quickly determine the interesting discoveries and begin to act on them.

The ability to export the nondata results and have them reused in custom applications is an important consideration. Many of the more sophisticated tools allow this to a greater or lesser degree. Typically, the tools allow SQL or C++ code segments to be exported for reuse in applications.

Because of the potentially large output data sets, vendors tend to provide the output data in the form of relational tables or a common interchangeable format for import to third-party relational or MDA tools. Tools that are well suited for large-volume data analysis have the following features:

❑ Display multidimensional cubes with slice and dice
❑ Rescale and resize graphics
❑ Drill down to data values from graphical views

Technical Considerations

Our discussion of the technical considerations criterion include openness, performance, and scalability as they relate to data mining tool selection.

Openness

A truly open data mining tool will have some of the following characteristics:

❑ **External application access**

External application access means access from applications to the data mining algorithms and services. Application access allows for the extension of existing user applications as well as the provision over time of vendor and third-party applications and solutions.

❑ **Output sharing**

Output sharing is the ability of the tool to share data and nondata output with other vendor tools and/or user applications. Included here is the ability of the tool itself to share output among its own set of techniques so that the output of one technique can be the input of another technique, where appropriate, of course.

❑ **Ability to read diverse data sources**

The tool must be able to read a diverse set of data sources and input formats, including flat files and relational and nonrelational databases.

❑ **Available on multiple platforms**

The tool should be available on the leading server platforms of several vendors.

Scalability

Although data mining is usually associated with processing large amounts of data, many algorithms today are limited in the amount of data they can process. This often reflects the academic background of the original development where volumes were smaller than those found in commercial environments (where the focus was not necessarily on performance). In addition, some techniques are inherently not very scalable. For example, some implementations of the associations discovery technique suffer because of the exponential increase in time needed to handle each new variable that is added to the mix.

Clearly, the ability to handle large data volumes in a scalable way is critical. Commercial organizations need to derive answers quickly from increasingly large databases and must do so without extensive sampling. Scalability must address not just the depth of the data but also its width. As the number of columns increases, many algorithms degrade significantly or simply stop after hitting an internal processing limitation. Linear scalability in both directions should be the objective. Here there are no magic answers. Our best advice is to look for a sound architecture, ideally a modern three-tier approach, and last but not least, availability of the tool on the leading symmetric multiprocessor (SMP) and massively parallel processor (MPP) platforms. Most importantly, get some customer testimonials.

Performance. Although performance is one of the key issues in the selection of a data mining tool, few, if any, independent benchmark figures are available to compare the raw throughput of competing vendor products. There is not yet a data mining equivalent of the Transaction Processing Council (TPC) figures that are so commonly quoted in the database world.

In general, the following factors affect the performance of a data mining tool:

❑ **Amount of data to be mined**

This factor is obvious, of course. Remember, however, that although data volumes in commercial data mining are usually large, often they can be substantially reduced by expert sampling, preprocessing, and data reduction techniques.

❑ **Particular data mining technique used**

Different algorithms have varying requirements in terms of data processing. For example, an associations discovery algorithm typically runs faster than a neural network, and an RBF neural network usually trains faster than a backpropagation neural network.

❑ **Number of variables specified**

All algorithms are affected by the amount of input to the task to be carried out. For example, the amount of effort to predict the creditworthiness of a customer will increase as the number of input variables increases.

❑ **Level of accuracy specified, if applicable**

Some data mining tools allow users to specify the level of confidence with which they want the resulting model to work. Greater accuracy means more fine-tuning by the data mining tool.

❑ **Whether flat files or databases are used**

In general, processing against flat files is faster than running against a database engine. Most tools allow for both options.

❑ **Capacity and architecture of the computer system used**

Clearly, capacity has a major impact on performance time, particularly where the tool and database are running in a parallel environment *and* they are both enabled to take advantage of the parallelism.

Conclusions

Obviously, tools are an essential part of any data mining armory, but on their own and without expert domain and technical knowledge, leveraging major advantage from them can be difficult. Even with the best tools, a tools-only strategy can easily run into any number of roadblocks—from the unusability of the tool to the lack of vision in applying the new knowledge to business problems.

Data Mining Applications

There are two broad categories of data mining applications: generic (cross-industry) and industry-specific. Data mining applications typically are sold with specific services to cover customization and to ensure a fast start for the customer.

Generic Applications

Many traditional applications of data mining technology address challenges that are felt across almost all industries. For example, the tasks of customer segmentation and database marketing are so commonly required that some vendors have found it worthwhile to develop suites of generic applications in these areas. Generic applications have the following advantages:

❑ They provide a quick start for the customer

❑ They are cost-effective when compared to custom development

❑ Their functional content is often sharply focused, especially if the application was developed originally in conjunction with a customer organization

Some examples of generic applications include Database Mining Marksman from HNC Software Inc. (targeted marketing), and DecisionEdge and Business Discovery Solutions (targeted marketing, campaign management), from IBM.

Industry-Specific Applications

Industry-specific applications are found primarily in the finance and retail industries, and their development has been driven by the long-established data mining practices in those industries.

Examples are IBM's Fraud and Abuse Management System (fraud detection for the healthcare and retail industries) and INTRA/Knowledge from Information Discovery Inc. (CRM and marketing analysis for the finance industry).

Conclusions

Data mining applications overcome some of the problems of a tools-only strategy. By offering a packaged solution, they simultaneously lower the skill requirements and focus attention on common business objectives through a generic or customizable interface. The result is frequently faster and more reliable ROIs.

Data Mining Services

All of the commercial data mining vendors offer data mining services. These services may range from product installation and training to a full-blown business intelligence consultancy engagement, as described below.

Consultancy Services

Consultancy services address data mining in the context of general business management, for example, as part of a program for business process reengineering or customer relationship management. This kind of consultancy is often called *business intelligence consultancy*. The consultants who perform the services typically have an industry-specific background and use a formal data mining methodology, ideally coupled with a management consultancy methodology. They are knowledgeable about a cross-section of approaches (both traditional and new) to solving business problems through data analysis and have exposure to different data mining tools and applications.

Consultancy services are typically offered only by the larger vendors, and although they are expensive, they have the clear advantage of guaranteeing a quick startup with excellent prospects of a fast and substantial ROI.

Implementation Services

Implementation services focus on how to implement a specific data mining solution. Small vendors may offer only installation, customization, and education on their products, whereas large vendors may provide a data mining team of analysts and a manager to drive the overall project (with, of course, involvement from the customer's business and technical resources). Be aware that some data mining tools are available exclusively through associated data mining implementation services. Two current examples are Solomon from Syllogic International B.V. in the Netherlands and SE-Learn / SE-Classify from Modeling Labs in Pittsburgh.

The price of and potential payback from implementation services increases as the service offering moves from simple product-based services to project engagement services.

Education Services

All vendors offer product-specific education and training, and some provide more general data mining education. The education ranges from one-day executive awareness programs to intensive workshops. The executive awareness programs offer a general description of the potential of data mining to solve business problems and to help to identify possible data mining applications in the customer's organization. The workshop programs focus, in addition, on detailed case studies, overviews of algorithms, and some hands-on work. (Although the case studies are typically based on generic data, in some cases it is possible for customers to work on in-house data, where confidentiality permits.) Some classes require the attendance of a minimum of two representatives from a customer organization to ensure adequate coverage of both the business and technical aspects of the mining solution.

Clearly, both the executive awareness and workshop programs offer an attractive kick-start to the prospective data mining team in a risk-free environment.

Related Services

Several services are related to data mining. For the novice data mining team, these services may represent uncharted waters. The related services are:

Data warehousing. These services are aimed at tackling a problem that is closely related to data mining—data warehouse planning and/or implementation. Typically, the providers of data warehousing services offer a proprietary data warehouse blueprint or architecture and combine that with an implementation methodology. A data warehouse typically is implemented though a combination of products from the vendor and several partners to ensure a best-of-breed implementation for an individual customer solution.

Data warehouse services are widely available and are offered by all of the major database vendors (IBM, Informix, Oracle, and Sybase) and some specialized companies (for example, Prism Solutions Inc.).

Data householding. These services are effectively a way of outsourcing much of the data preparation step of the data mining process, and they have become popular in recent years with the growth of data warehousing and data mining. Several specialized companies operate data warehousing services, two of which are SHL Systemhouse and Axiom in the United States.

Data syndication. These services provide sources of external data to the data mining project. Typical examples are credit scoring data and demographic and psychographic data.

Two well-known U.S.-based providers in this area are A.C. Nielsen and the U.S. Census Bureau.

Conclusions

Data mining services offer even greater leverage than a tools-only or tools-and-application strategy. This leverage from services increases the earlier in the data mining process the service is used, with business intelligence consultancy services offering the greatest opportunities. Such services typically include a strong business perspective, industry-specific data mining expertise, a choice of applications and tools, and a tried-and-tested data mining methodology. They are a fast way of bringing to the data mining endeavor a level of expertise that would be difficult or impossible to hire into the organization and that would substantially increase the potential payback on investment. See "Getting Started with Data Mining" on page 125 for a more detailed discussion on this topic.

Part 3
Implementation

6

Case Studies

Good judgment comes from experience. Experience comes from bad judgment.
(Philippe Muller)

In this chapter we describe two case studies where data mining has been applied to common business-critical problems. The cases have been chosen primarily because of the broad applicability of their approaches and the variety of data mining operations and techniques used.

The case studies are based on actual projects, and the organizations that own the projects have kindly allowed their names to be retained. Naturally, some details have been omitted for the sake of clarity. The projects were carried out under very specific circumstances that may or may not apply to your environment. In addition, they were devised and run by qualified professionals in both the relevant business domain and data mining technology. The message should be clear at this stage: Do not try this at home and expect to get the same results without adequate supervision!

Preventing Fraud and Abuse

This case study describes the application of data mining to tackle two objectives, which apply across most industries:

❑ Identification of potential fraud and/or potential abuse

❑ Identification of generic groupings of clients from a large and diverse client base

The case demonstrates the ability of data mining to deliver new business insights and substantial monetary returns in areas where traditional techniques had not been successful.

Background

The Health Insurance Commission (HIC) in Australia is a federal government agency in the business of public and private health insurance administration. The HIC pays insurance claims from more than 20 million Australians and pays out about A$8 billion in funds every year. More than 300 million transactions are processed and stored every year, yielding an online claims database of approximately 550GB and a five-year history claims database of about 1.3TB (1,300GB).

One of HIC's programs is Fraud and Inappropriate Practice Prevention. Through frequent and regular contact, HIC has developed an excellent collaborative relationship with its general practitioners (GPs) of medicine. The twice yearly contacts supply the GPs with detailed reports on how their practices compare with those of GPs in similar practices across the country. The approach is aimed at modifying GP behavior to promote better medical practices rather than at investigating and prosecuting GPs, although both strategies are employed.

Business Objectives Identification

The healthcare industry around the world has faced a steady increase in costs over the last couple of years. To ensure their survival, industry participants are trying to figure out ways of controlling and reducing these costs.

The focus of the HIC project was on the recent and steady 10% annual rise in the cost of pathology claims for clinical tests. The overall business objective of the project was to find a way to ensure that medical pathology tests were prescribed appropriately without negatively affecting the services provided by the GPs.

The HIC decided on a two-fold approach: first, to identify potential fraudulent claims or claims arising from inappropriate practice and, second, to develop general profiles of the GP practices in order to compare practice behaviors of individual GPs.

Inappropriate practice is defined as the prescribing of unnecessary, unreasonable, or exaggerated services. It should be stressed that the vast majority of GPs are honest and have their patients' best interests at heart. In fact, outright fraud is not likely to occur frequently, given the tight controls that surround the claims payment system. Nevertheless, some GPs might use medical services in a way that does not produce the best outcome for the available funding.

Data Preparation

The required data was selected from two databases: an episode database (where an episode is a single consultation between a patient and a GP) and a GP database. All work was based on a subset of data for the State of New South Wales, and it related to the years 1994 and 1995. Figure 31 on page 108 shows an overview of the general approach taken during the project.

The episode database contained 6.8 million records, one for each patient visit. Each record contained up to 20 pathology tests, which the GP ordered as a result of the visit. There were 227 different pathology tests. To this data were added several additional descriptive details such as age and sex of the GP making a total of 120 variables per record available for analysis.

The GP database contained 17,000 records that related to the active GPs during the time period under investigation. This database was aggregated, and the HIC project team then added several descriptive variables, such as age and sex of the GP. A total of 105 variables were available for analysis.

The GP profiling was to be done using a neural segmentation algorithm, an approach that necessitated some special data preparation. Because the episode database records held up to 20 test requests, the records had to be pivoted and then aggregated by provider (GP) ID. The behavior of 10,409 GPs was to be studied. The result was a matrix of 10,409 by 227 elements, where each element represented the numbers of each test ordered by each of the GPs. The elements were then scaled from 0 to 1 with respect to the total number of tests of each kind. Figure 32 on page 109 illustrates the general structure of the final input records.

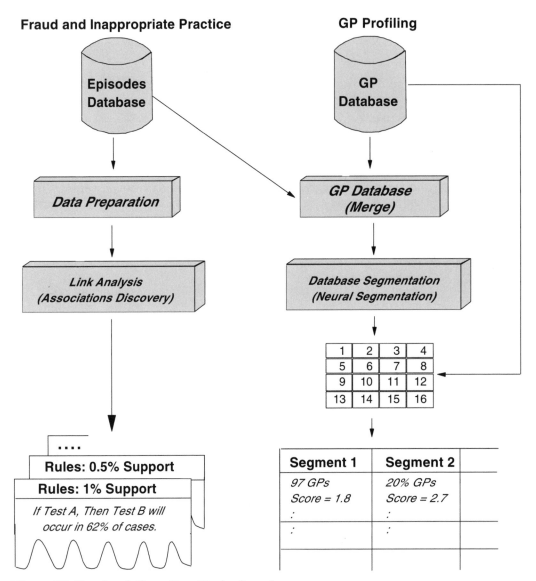

Figure 31. Fraud and Abuse Case Study: Overview

Data Mining

The identification of fraud and inappropriate practice was done by applying link analysis (using an associations discovery operation) to the episode database. The approach was to run the operation several times, with each successive run looking for more deep-seated rules, that is, rules that were supported by a smaller and smaller number of records. (Deep-seated rules often provide business value but can also pick up spurious associations that reflect nothing more than noise in the database.) To guard against potentially worthless rules, a confidence level of 50% was set for all runs; that is, the team was interested only in rules that held true at least 50% of the time. Figure 34 on page 110 depicts the user input screen for specifying the data sources and controlling parameters.

Provider ID	Test 1	Test 2	Test 3	...	Test 227
Provider 1	0.02	0.00	0.11	...	0.00
Provider 2	0.00	0.05	0.01	...	0.00
Provider 3	0.02	0.12	0.00	...	0.00
...	...	...	...	...	...
Provider 10,409	0.00	0.02	0.00	0.18	0.00

Figure 32. *Fraud and Abuse Case Study: Input to Neural Segmentation*

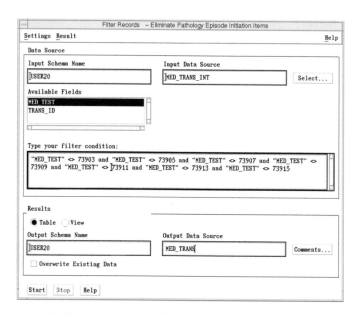

Figure 33. *Fraud and Abuse Case Study: Filtering Out the PEI Codes*

As the level of support was reduced in successive runs from 1% to 0.5% and then to 0.25%, the number of discovered rules increased accordingly. At each run the team observed several interesting and potentially actionable rules. However, at the 0.25% support level, the team decided that the presence of some tests in the input database was causing spurious rules to be revealed. These tests, generally known as Pathology Episode Initiation (PEI) tests, attracted fees that varied depending on who ordered them and where they were ordered. When the PEI tests were removed from the run, the number of rules dropped significantly, thus providing much greater clarity in the remaining rules. (In fact, it was from the remaining rules that the most commercially valuable discoveries were later made.) Figure 35 on page 111 illustrates the number of rules that were found at different levels of support, both before and after the removal of the PEI test records. Figure 33 on page 109 illustrates the user screen for filtering out the PEI tests before rerunning the associations operation.

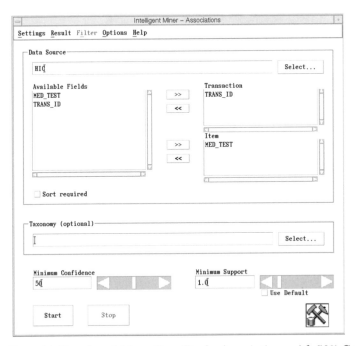

Figure 34. *Fraud and Abuse Case Study: Associations with 50% Confidence and 1% Support*

The team did the GP profiling in two phases: the pivoted subset from the episode database was segmented, and the resulting segments were then overlaid by descriptive details from the GP database to augment

Support Level	1%	0.5%	0.25%	1% (no PEI)
Number of Rules	24	64	135	9

Figure 35. *Fraud and Abuse Case Study: Rules at 50% Confidence Level*

the descriptions of the segments. The GP database contained a classification for each GP which HIC had developed previously using neural networks. Hence, the team was interested in understanding how the current segmentation would relate to the existing classification.

The initial work was done by database segmentation. The underlying neural net was trained iteratively with 25 passes of the input data. The nature of the operation allowed the data mining team to select in advance the number of required output segments. The team decided on 16 segments, to which all records would then be mapped; that is, the operation would derive up to 16 different practice types and assign each of the 10,409 GPs to one of the practice types.

After the segmentation, the GP database was consulted to tag each of its records with the ID of the segment into which the corresponding GP best fit. This tagging enabled the team to derive additional descriptive information from the set of GPs in each segment; for example, the team computed the mean, standard deviation, maximum, and minimum for variables such as percentage of female patients, number of house calls, and age of GP. The net effect was a comprehensive characterization of each practice type.

Analysis of Results and Assimilation of Knowledge

Both the link analysis and GP profiling produced interesting results, the more insightful and understandable of which are summarized here.

The link analysis revealed interesting rules at each of the support levels at which it was run. The initial run with 1% support revealed, for example, that if a Multiple Biochemical Analysis (MBA) test was ordered, a Full Blood Examination (FBE) was also ordered in 62% of cases. This was a surprising finding.

Further runs at lower levels of support showed that there was a strong, persistent tendency among some GPs to order FBE and MBA tests as a type of catch-all strategy. Furthermore, these tests were frequently ordered (sometimes in up to 80% or 90% of cases) even when more specific tests were ordered at the same time. Although the appropriateness of using these tests in combination can be judged only by medical authorities, the results show that a significant proportion of

GPs habitually ordered general screening tests rather than spending time with their patients to develop clinical diagnoses based on individual patient histories.

The most significant results, however, were uncovered after the PEI tests were removed from the database and the number of rules was reduced from 135 to 9. The analysis revealed that a request for a microscopic examination of feces for parasites (OCP) was associated with a cultural examination of feces (FCS) in 0.86% of cases. This rule was the norm, with a 92.6% chance that if OCP tests were requested, they would be done with FCS. However, another rule stated that, in 0.61% of cases, OCP was associated with a different, more expensive, test called *MCS2*. Although there was no bar against ordering the MCS2 test, this was clearly out-of-line with expectations, and there can be little doubt that the great majority of these cases represented an unnecessary upcoding of the test that was actually required. The financial incentive to order the MCS2 test instead of the FCS test was A$13.55 per test. This represented a potential overpayment in New South Wales alone of more than A$500,000 per year.

The GP profiling produced 16 practice profiles, which are summarized in Figure 36 on page 113.

Each segment is labeled to reflect the essential characteristics of the underlying practice type and includes the total number of GPs within that segment, the average number of tests they ordered, and their average neural network score (where a lower score indicates greater likelihood of fraud or inappropriate practice).

A review of the segments makes interesting reading. For example, consider segment 13, which represents the majority of traditional GPs who are practicing conventionally. This segment, with 5450 members, represents 52% of the GP population, yet it accounts for only 6.2% of the medical pathology tests. Contrast this with segment 4, with 54 members, which represents 0.51% of the GPs but accounts for 2.7% of the tests. The difference in the average neural net score between segments 13 and 4 is striking.

1: Cancer Treatment	2: GPs Practicing in the Country	3: Extended Hours Clinic	4: Self Professed Experts
97 GPs Class 1.8 3.6% of total tests ordered 4347 average tests/GP Manage cancer patients with or without proper training and supervision	206 GPs Class 2.7 4.8% of total tests ordered 2733 average tests/GP GPs practicing in the country, doing less pathology and when done, these are often obstetrics tests	102 GPs Class 1.8 4.8% 4537 average tests/GP Extended hours clinic	54 GPs Class 1.3 2.7% 5736 average tests/GP Self professed experts outside mainstream (e.g., chronic fatigue)
5: Average Tests	**6: Over Servicing Bad**	**7: Over Servicing Less Bad**	**8: Average GP - Acupuncture**
445 GPs Class 2.4 8.4% 2204 average tests/GP	149 GPs Class 1.7 4.8% 3745 average tests/GP "Classic" over servicing - bad	151 GPs Class 2.0 4.4% 3422 average tests/GP "Classic" over servicing-less bad	442 GPs Class 2.3 8.7% 2288 average tests/GP "Average GP" using acupuncture
9: Older GPs	**10: Environmental Medicine**	**11: Young GPs**	**12: AIDS, STD, Drug Clinics**
1735 GPs Class 2.7 18.5% 1240 average tests/GP Older GPs with small practices	127 GPs Class 1.8 4% 3677 average tests/GP Environmental medicine	227GPs Class 2.5 5.1% 2631 average tests/GP Young GPs in acute medical clinics	26 GPs Class 1.9 0.8% 3471 average tests/GP AIDS, STD, drug addiction clinics
13: Body of GPs	**14: Geriatric Practice**	**15: Female GPs**	**16: Young Female GPs**
5450 GPs Class 2.8 6.2% 433 average tests/GP Body of GPs represent conventional general practice (many part time)	500 GPs Class 2.2 11.2% 2604 average tests/GP Geriatric practice	595 GPs Class 2.9 9.2% 1802 average tests/GP Female GPs working on female health	103 GPs Class 2.2 3.7% 4166 average tests/GP Young female GPs in women's health clinics

Figure 36. Fraud and Abuse Case Study: GP Profiles

Summary of Findings and Benefits

Clearly, the project was successful in terms of producing several findings that were previously unknown, valid, and actionable.

The link analysis provided an immediate opportunity for substantial cost savings to the tune of A$500,000 in one state alone and raised the prospect of additional savings in other states. This upcoding problem remained undetected for five years by conventional techniques. In addition, the analysis provided a perspective on the different ordering patterns and behaviors of GPs that had not been possible before. Finally, the analysis suggests many further avenues of exploration, perhaps more than the HIC can fully handle, given its limited resources.

The GP profiling revealed detailed subpopulations within the GP population that had not been known previously. Several manual efforts in this area were unsuccessful. The new profiles have enabled the HIC to improve the focus and value of its GP communications program as well as increase the effectiveness of its Fraud and Inappropriate Practice Prevention efforts.

The key benefit of the project has been to enable the HIC to improve its services while at the same time effectively control rising costs. This project is a good example of the HIC's innovative approach to cost control, which has helped keep Australian healthcare costs at 8.5% of the gross domestic product (GDP), compared to, for example, 15% of the GDP in the United States.

Improving Direct Mail Responses

This case study tackles the common and continued problem of poor response rates to direct mail campaigns. Response rates can be as low as 1% or 2%. Clearly, at these low levels of response, even a small improvement can significantly enhance the ROI, part of which comes from the savings in marketing materials and distribution expenses.

Background

Mellon Bank Corporation is a major financial services company headquarted in Pittsburgh, Pennsylvania. Its two core businesses are investment services and banking services.

In recent years, Mellon has strengthened its position in the financial services industry through integrating strategic acquisitions, reconfiguring consumer businesses and delivery systems, continuing its commitment to expanding trust and investment management services, and building relationships to better serve corporate customers.

Mellon has always been at the forefront of advanced technology and was an early adopter of computer technology in banking. That tradition continues today with about $350 million invested each year in computer technology.

Business Objectives Identification

Management at Mellon is well aware of the value of leveraging its customer information both within and among its various lines of business. A major focus area has been lifetime customer value, and the company has adopted a methodology to develop models to predict the potential lifetime value to the bank of a customer—from initial prospect to new customer, and, it is hoped, to life-long customer of the bank.

Figure 37 illustrates the life cycle for the takeup and use of a loan product from the bank.

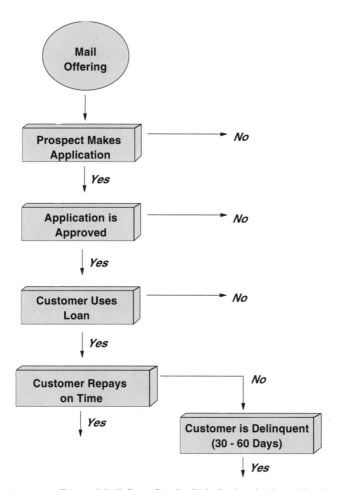

Figure 37. *Direct Mail Case Study: Life Cycle of a Loan Product*

Clearly, these life-cycle models are not simple in real life, and each phase is itself a potentially complex submodel. There may well be 10 or 12 of these submodels in the overall life-cycle.

The Mellon data mining team had a general business objective to develop a life cycle model for one of its products, a home equity line of credit (HELOC), which is essentially an extendible loan secured by the value of a client's own property.

Specifically, this case deals with the first step in building the overall life-cycle model—building a model for the initial direct mailing phase. Clearly, the objective was to ensure the highest possible ROI from the mailing. Achieving that would necessitate not just securing a high response rate but also getting responses that were likely to lead to high lifetime value.

Figure 38 illustrates the general approach the team took. The prospects for the mailing were the existing demand deposit account (DDA) customers, and the model for a good prospect was to be the subset of the DDA customers who already had bought a HELOC product. The approach was to generalize the in-house experience with existing customers who had both a HELOC and DDA and to predict which DDA-only customers were likely to be the most profitable long-term prospects.

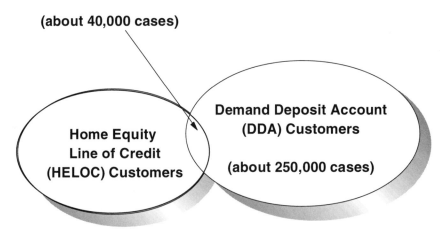

Figure 38. *Direct Mail Case Study: The Business Objective*

Data Preparation

The data preparation phase presented several challenges, among them the multiplicity of data sources, lack of historical information in many cases, need to restructure some of the input data, and sensitivity of some of the selected variables.

Given the focus on DDA customers, a primary data source was the approximately 40,000 Mellon customers who had (or once had) both HELOCs and DDAs. This data was supplemented with demographic and home property information from the in-house marketing database and from external sources. The key data sources (and some of their variables) were:

- ❏ DDA data (history of loan balance over 3, 6, 9, 12, and 18 months, history of returned checks, history of interest rates)

- ❏ Demographic data sourced both internally and externally (age, income, length of residence, and other indicators of economic condition)

- ❏ Property data sourced externally (home purchase price, loan-to-value ratio)

- ❏ Other data related to credit worthiness

In addition to the above sources, information about known responses to previous mailings was added to the mix. After considering various combinations of variables and extensive statistical analysis, the team finally settled on a set of some 120 variables. (In general it is not simple to evaluate the best variables for direct response mailing as, typically, little is known about the prospects before they actually take up the offer and become customers. Contrast this with prediction of attrition or delinquency where the characteristics and historical behavior of the subjects are much better understood.)

Less than one-half of the DDAs had history records associated with them. In addition, because of the multiple sources of data, many of the final input records were sparsely filled. The team had to drop the inadequate DDA records and sparse records from the analysis.

In addition, the DDA records were structured into household folders, so the team had to decompose the folders into individual account records for presentation to the mining algorithms.

Finally, the team had to be careful not to include such variables as age, sex, or race on which any decision to make an offer might be based. Mellon also had to ensure compliance with legal restrictions regarding the use of credit worthiness data.

Data Mining

The general approach was to use predictive modeling (using a value prediction operation based on RBFs). Figure 39 on page 118 shows an overview of the approach. Predictive models are developed in two distinct phases: training and testing. In this case, the team trained the model on the augmented DDA records and the resulting trained model (called the *Response Model*) was then used in test mode to rank each of the prospects in terms of likelihood to respond. The team then carried out several visualization and cross-validation procedures.

For the training phase, the DDA records were selected randomly from the data set, which at the time had been reduced to some 45,000 valid records. However, the selections were heavily weighted to include

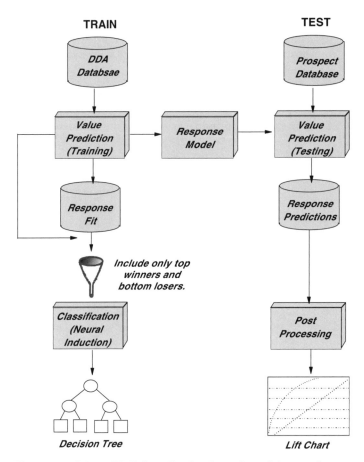

Figure 39. Direct Mail Case Study: Overview of Approach

many more responders than would be normal in a random selection, to give the data mining algorithm more exposure to what is normally a very rare occurrence. (The novice may consider this akin to cheating, but it is quite normal practice in these cases.) Figure 40 on page 119 illustrates the user screen for selecting the variables and specifying various controlling parameters for the training phase.

The resulting ranked records (called the *response fit*) were analyzed to understand the rationale for ranking that the value prediction algorithm had used. This analysis was aimed at validating the predictions. The validation was done by using a special visualization tool, which effectively applied database segmentation to the 10% of records that were most likely to respond (*winners*) and the 10% that were least likely to respond (*losers*). This technique enabled the team to better understand the most important factors in the underlying predictive

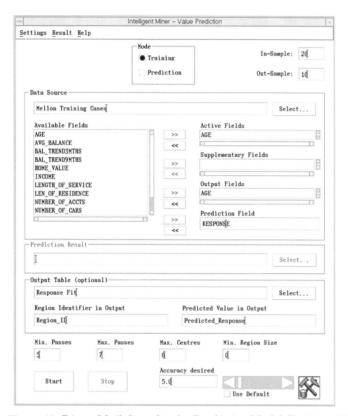

Figure 40. *Direct Mail Case Study: Predictive Model Training Phase*

model. Secondary validation was done by presenting the winners and losers to a classification algorithm. This algorithm developed a decision tree to explain graphically the rationale behind the rankings. Effectively the algorithm was given the predicted outcome for each record and was asked to develop a rationale for this classification. The actual ranking was held in a variable called WINLOSE, which could hold two possible values: *W* for winners and *L* for losers. Figure 41 on page 120 illustrates the user screen used to run this classification.

For the testing phase, the team repeatedly sampled the prospects database. This time the samples represented the unweighted, normal concentration of likely and unlikely responders. The model produced in the training phase was used to rank each of the prospects. After the prospects were ranked, the rankings were validated. For the validation the team used statistical techniques and a charting device called a lift chart or a *gains chart*.

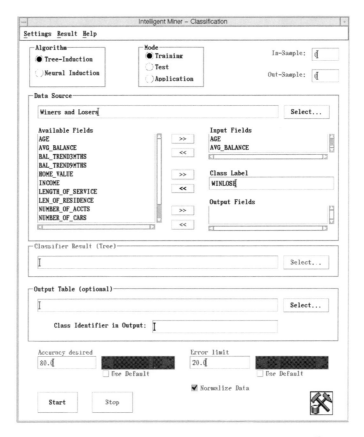

Figure 41. *Direct Mail Case Study: Building the Decision Tree*

Of course, several iterations of the training and testing phases were needed before the team settled on a model.

Analysis of Results and Assimilation of Knowledge

The results of the work are best illustrated by the lift chart from the analysis (see Figure 42 on page 121). In this case the lift chart was used to demonstrate the benefits of a mailing to only the more likely responders as opposed to a random mailing to all prospects.

It is worth spending a little time to fully understand the lift chart.

The basic idea is that, in random mailing, the number of likely respondents increases only linearly with the number of letters sent. For example, if the bank solicits 25% of its prospects, it will hit 25% of the responders in the total prospect set; if it solicits 50%, it will hit 50% of

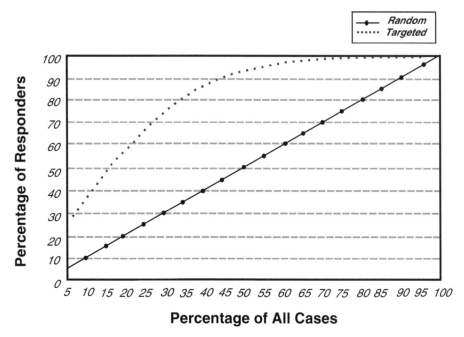

Figure 42. Direct Mail Case Study: Lift Chart

the responders; and so on. Mellon Bank can do substantially better than linear, however, by targeting the mailing to the more likely respondents. The lift chart illustrates the increased response (or lift) that is possible at different levels of mailing coverage. (The chart is built by sorting the ranked prospects' records into descending order, dividing them into quantiles, and plotting them cumulatively.)

The results of the mining show that Mellon could expect to attract more than 90% of the responders by mailing to only 50% of the prospects. Obviously, mailing more prospects would attract even more responses, but the ROI trails off significantly at higher levels of coverage.

Another key result of the analysis was an insight into the kinds of customers who are more likely to accept (or reject) the solicitation. Figure 43 on page 122 illustrates the decision tree produced for the analysis.

The circles (nodes) represent decision points along the path to a terminal square (leaf), where all of the prospects that took that path are grouped. Some leaves hold the winners, and some hold the losers. The team analyzed several of the groups in turn, some winners and some losers. Tracing a path from the top node to the bottom leaf reveals the set of decision rules that determined the assignment of a particular

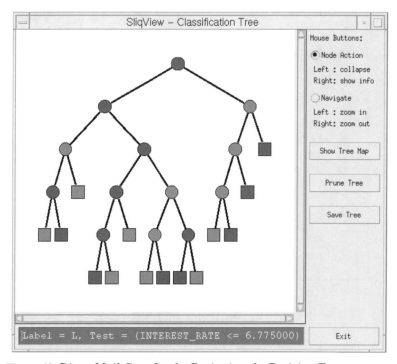

Figure 43. *Direct Mail Case Study: Reviewing the Decision Tree*

prospect to that particular leaf. One group that was analyzed (indicated by the mouse pointer in Figure 43) represented more than 1,500 prospects, all of whom were predicted to be winners. Figure 44 illustrates the decision rules associated with this group.

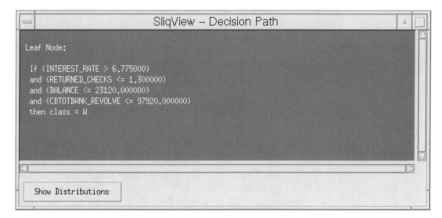

Figure 44. *Direct Mail Case Study: Reviewing the Decision Rules*

Clearly, for this group, an INTEREST_RATE greater than 6.775% is the most important deciding factor in accepting the offer, followed by several less important factors such as number of returned checks and the total DDA balance. This analysis offered the bank a detailed insight into the decision-making process which makes certain groups of prospects either more or less likely to accept a mailing.

Summary of Findings and Benefits

This project enabled Mellon Bank to immediately and substantially increase the leverage of its direct mailing campaigns and produced several side-benefits that will yield important advantages in the long term.

The ability to increase the leverage of the direct mailing campaign arose from the output of the predictive models, which highlighted the most likely respondents on the basis of historically observed customer behavior. More importantly, it became clear that 90% of the best prospects, for example, could be reached by mailing to only 50% of the prospects. In other words, the bank discovered not just a smaller target audience but one that was also likely to have a higher lifetime value. Although the bank could only realize the full lifetime benefits over time, it experienced immediate savings being able to mail to only a limited prospect list. Mellon was in a position to substantially reduce mailing costs in a controlled fashion to meet budgetary restraints. For example, it could have limited the mailing to 20% of the prospect list, anticipating reaching more than 50% of the responders.

In addition, using the decision tree to visualize the profiles of good and poor responders helped the bank to prepare different solicitation letters for different subgroups in the prospect list.

One of the side-benefits of the project is worthy of comment. The team noted that the predictive models did not use some of the data that had been purchased externally. Thus, there was no need to continue to pay for these variables, and savings were made here too.

Finally, and perhaps most importantly in terms of long-term benefits, the project sharply highlighted the huge effort required to prepare the data in contrast to the relatively small effort required for the actual data mining. This benefit, in turn, has prompted a heightened interest in a strategic approach to data gathering and cleansing before data mining—in other words, a data warehouse.

7

Getting Started with Data Mining

*If we are to perceive all of the implications of
the new, we must risk, at least temporarily,
ambiguity and disorder.*
(J. J. Gordon)

In this chapter we offer advice and guidance to the newcomer who is
contemplating getting started with data mining. To help you establish
whether data mining is likely to fit into your organization and to
assess your level of readiness for it, we start with a data mining readiness assessment and a review of some of the key issues in data mining
today. Both will reveal a lot about the appropriateness of data mining
for your organization and how ready your organization is to embrace
it. Then, assuming you are still following the debate, we offer a general approach for getting started. Finally, we discuss some of the key
decisions to be made in getting started, focusing on costs, timescales,
and critical success factors.

Are You Ready for Data Mining?

Let's start with some basic questions. Is your organization in an industry where data mining already has an established track record? Are your competitors already involved in data mining or planning to get involved? Most importantly, does your organization have the basic prerequisites for data mining?

Today, the industries where data-driven solutions to business intelligence tend to be best established are typically those where there are large volumes of data and/or a high degree of organizational complexity with any number of complicating factors such as international operations or a wide variety of markets served. These industries are characterized by long traditions of computerization and a focus on data-driven decision making. Hence, we find that many of the leading examples of data warehousing and data mining today are in the banking and insurance industries. The retail industry is also a strong proponent, largely because of the increasingly competitive environment, low profit margins, and the ready supply of relatively clean data that is captured automatically at POS terminals. More recently, because of a worldwide movement toward deregulation of formerly monopolistic utility services, we find an increasing number of telecommunications and other public utility companies entering the data mining fray.

Organizations that have embraced data mining are themselves often leaders in their respective industries. Some examples are Bank of America, and AT&T. Data mining is not the sole preserve of these large industry leaders, however. Any organization that possesses these essential ingredients is open to data mining:

❑ **A culture of innovation**

The organization is open to new and creative ways of doing business. It constantly strives for better customer relations, improved product quality, and innovative customer services and is aware of the data-driven path to success in keeping abreast of the competition. This implies a willingness to change business practices and processes in order to act on the results from the data mining analysis. While this may seem obvious, in practice change is not so easy.

❑ **A paradigm shift**

The organization is approaching some fundamental changes in the way it does business—for example, industry deregulation, a merger, a new market opportunity, or, indeed, a fight for its very survival. All of these situations will easily evoke new and creative ways of managing the business and provide a rich breeding ground for the adoption of data mining solutions.

❑ **An in-house champion**

Whether an organization is positioning itself to leapfrog the competition or simply struggling for survival, an internal champion of data mining is critical. Such sponsorship typically comes from the ranks of executive management or from middle managers with an analytical background.

Challenges

Data mining has its fair share of challenges. They range from technical and business issues to the possibly more consequential social issues that are beginning to emerge as the practice of data mining gains more widespread use and exposure.

Social Issues

In general, social issues receive far less scrutiny than the business and technical issues, yet in many ways the social consequences of data mining may be far more profound.

The most noted work in this area is the set of principles protecting individual privacy drawn up by the Organization for Economic Cooperation and Development (OECD). The principles relate directly to anyone working with data mining in general, and specifically to work that deals with traceable, individual data records. They cover such aspects as the openness of records to individual scrutiny, the fairness and legality with which the data is collected, and, perhaps most importantly for data mining, the requirement to specify in *advance* the purpose for which the data is being collected and to restrict usage to that specific purpose. These latter requirements would appear to place the use of legacy databases outside the scope of data mining projects. Equally, the requirement to limit the use to some originally specified one would probably preclude the data miner from analyzing consolidated databases. As most data mining today is based on legacy and consolidated data sources, the OECD principles clearly have major implications for data mining practitioners. Currently, 24 countries, including Australia, the United Kingdom, and the United States, have adopted the principles to some degree and effecting legislation has been passed.

Given the extent to which both proprietary and syndicated databases are shared, consolidated, and mined today, it is easy to explain the growing public concern over the so-called big-brother-is-watching-you effect presented in George Orwell's *1984*.

Business Issues

The business issues are related to the ability of the organization to translate the data mining results into meaningful business actions. Recalling our definition of data mining, the discovered information must be *previously unknown, valid,* and *actionable*—a tall order for any data miner even with today's mining tools.

Several business factors tend to get in the way of coming up with a winning result. For example, all predictive analysis is done on the basis of historically observed activity. Thus customer purchasing predictions are based on analysis of choices customers *have* made, not on choices they *may* make. Although choices are presumed to reveal information about customer preferences, choices and preferences are not equivalent. Preferences are more stable than choices, but there is usually no information about preferences (unless a survey has been conducted explicitly for this purpose). In addition, it is unlikely that an organization will have legacy data on attitudes, perceptions, and the availability of competitive offerings. The past is not always a good predictor of the future.

A common issue is the problem of attaching real business value to the new information. In the search for truly unknown information, analysts are tempted to lower the level of confidence with which the data mining tools will report findings. In these situations, analysts often end up asking themselves whether the information truly has statistical significance or reflects only a one-off occurrence due to overmining of the data.

Finally, the ability to integrate the new data mining solution into existing business procedures and applications is critical to making the mining a repeatable, streamlined process that will help build the necessary culture of data-driven business intelligence.

Technical Issues

Several technical issues, ranging from poor data quality to lack of cooperation from overly possessive in-house data owners, beset the data miner.

By far the greatest problem in the technical arena is poor data quality. Typically the selected data is noisy (has missing and/or invalid data contents) and is stored in complex data structures designed more for operational efficiency than for data mining. Large data volumes exacerbate the problem. Even if data is sourced from outside the organization, the challenge remains of consolidating such syndicated data with in-house sources into a consistent, reliable analytical model for mining purposes.

The political problem of getting access to in-house data sources is common in many mining projects, given the typical requirement to source the data from diverse databases.

Furthermore, in addition to large numbers of records, data miners are frequently faced with large numbers of variables in each record. Increasing numbers of variables exponentially complicates the work of the mining tool.

Two additional technical concerns are the scope and depth of skills needed to drive the data mining project (good data mining skills are rare, and even rarer when coupled with industry knowledge) and the relative immaturity of this marketplace today (no standards for comparing facilities, performance, or model accuracy). These issues are discussed in more detail in "Assessing Vendor Solutions" on page 136 and "Skills and Timescales" on page 136.

Planning Your Approach

If you are still reading this chapter, then you are clearly in an industry and organization that are ready for data mining and are convinced that none of the issues will present insurmountable problems. In that case, the next step is to plan your overall approach. Figure 45 on page 130 shows a general approach to the task of getting started.

The approach shows an initial, one-off orientation step, which is followed by an iterative cycle of project definition, execution, and integration as the organization rolls out successive projects.

Let us look at the steps in detail:

❑ **Orientation**

The orientation process must develop an awareness of the business benefits and implications of data mining among management and influential technical professionals with a view to securing visibility and sponsorship for the idea. Some useful resources here are the emerging set of data mining books for business readers (like this one and those in the bibliography), data warehouse and data mining conferences (even the annual U.S.-based International Conference on Knowledge Discovery and Data Mining is becoming more accessible to less academic audiences) and, of course, the World Wide Web (most data mining tool vendors offer general introductions to the subject on their sites).

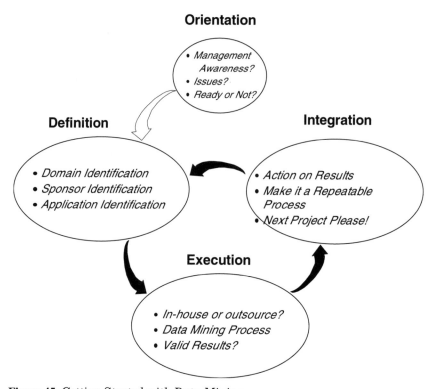

Figure 45. *Getting Started with Data Mining*

In addition, the orientation must include a review of the issues and challenges arising from data mining with respect to your organization so that you can make some initial high-level judgments about the applicability of the approach to your environment and, more importantly, your state of readiness to get going. The review will address such organizational considerations as who will sponsor the initiative, who owns the business case, and whether you need a data warehouse first.

❑ **Definition**

The objective here is to establish the domain and general objectives for the application, and to decide the broad approach to the project.

The domain is the general business area to which the application applies—market management, risk management, or fraud management (see). A combination of the domain and application objectives will help to identify an appropriate sponsor for the project. A good sponsor will provide the vision and political drive that is typically needed to carry through innovative projects in new areas. Frequently the application will already be well understood, in which case detailed business objectives are drawn up at this point. Otherwise a good candidate for a project should be selected along the lines suggested in "Selecting a Candidate Application" on page 133.

The definition step contains two of the key ingredients for successful data mining—good sponsorship and focused business objectives.

❑ **Execution**

The objective here clearly is to build the data mining application. Organizations that are new to data mining will have to decide, especially in the case of a first-time project, between an in-house project, an outsourced contract, or some hybrid of these. See "In-House or Outsource?" on page 134 for a discussion of the advantages and disadvantages of these options. Physically, what happens in the execution step depends largely on whether the project is outsourced or in-house. In either case, much time will be spent selecting and preprocessing the data before actual data mining can begin. Typically the preprocessing and mining will take several iterations before any reasonable conclusions can be drawn and, indeed, may necessitate returning to the definition phase.

❑ **Integration**

The integration step deals with the need to capitalize on the success of the project by integrating the results into the business and technical infrastructures of the organization. In practical terms, this means making the mining experience a repeatable, streamlined process. The intent is to have data mining, over time, become part of the way of doing business for the organization, and to develop a data-aware culture.

Technically, during this step, plans must be made for integrating the mining results (for example, business actions, databases, and predictive models) into the business and operational systems environment. Integration may involve new campaigns to exploit the business opportunity or head off the exposure, and plans to upgrade operational systems and adequately track the results arising from the business actions. For those organizations that are new to the data-driven approach to business intelligence, the integration step should provide momentum to move existing informational systems to a more strategic architecture through, for example, data warehousing.

Finally, truly successful data mining should always prompt the question, What next? And the cycle repeats itself.

In the remainder of this chapter we discuss in detail some of the key decision points in the general approach described above.

The Business Case

No project would be complete without a cost-benefit analysis, and data mining projects are no different. However, whereas most business cases suffer from real costs matched by intangible benefits, data mining projects are typically even more difficult to quantify in advance on the benefits side, given their exploratory nature. In addition, details on successful projects are hard to come by as few are willing to share their secrets. Often, data mining projects are justified by statements of broad business objectives such as: reduce the percentage of customer attrition by 5%, increase the response to direct mailings by 3%, or increase the profitability of a demand deposit customer by 10%.

Graham (1996) offers some interesting insights into project cost-benefits in the related area of data warehousing. Of the 62 organizations studied, the data warehouse projects showed an average ROI of 401%, but a huge variability in ROI ranging from minus 2,000% to plus 16,000% over the 2.3 year period under study—proof positive of the potentially exponential returns from a strategic approach to business intelligence.

Turning to the costs of getting started in data mining, we have already noted that the typical entry costs are high. The factors to consider are:

❑ **Outsourced projects**

Clearly outsourced projects can vary enormously, but initial projects will typically be in the $50,000 (usually just proof-of-concept) to $300,000 range.

❑ **Data mining tools**

You will find data mining tools in the marketplace in almost every price range. Some tools are distributed as freeware. Some PC-based products will cost no more than a few hundred dollars, though others can cost several tens of thousands of dollars. In general, multitask tools with good usability and scalability are expensive, especially on the popular SMP and MPP platforms. Some tools running on large UNIX or NT platforms can cost from $100,000 to $150,000.

❑ **Hardware**

Most data mining tools available today will run on standard hardware platforms. Popular platforms for these tools are high-end PCs; Sun, Hewlett Packard, IBM, DEC, and Silicon Graphics workstations; and IBM RS/6000 servers. Very few of the tools are restricted to one or two platforms only.

Clearly, as data volumes increase, most vendors will recommend that the tools be run on the high-end or special floating-point models within these platforms, with the associated increases in cost.

❑ **Data mining consultancy services**

Consultancy services are the quickest route to successful data mining, but good skills are still a rare commodity. Experienced practitioners command premium rates.

Some vendors offer a packaged data mining solution, including hardware, software, and services. One vendor currently offers such a solution at three levels: user solution ($10,000-$15,000), departmental solution ($150,000-$450,000), and enterprise solution ($500,000-$2,000,000).

Selecting a Candidate Application

In this section we present some key criteria by which to judge the contenders for your first or next data mining application. This discussion assumes that the application is a *real* business application and not a prototype (in which case some of the criteria, for example, the business case and the business objectives, would probably be relaxed a little).

The key selection criteria are:

❑ There is a **sponsor** for the application.

❑ The **business case** for the application is clearly understood and measurable, and the objectives are likely to be achievable given the resources that are being applied. (Equally, beware of very narrowly defined objectives that may represent a biased view of the problem.)

❑ The application has a high likelihood of having a **significant impact** on the business problem or opportunity at hand.

❑ Business **domain knowledge** is available.

❑ **Good quality, relevant data** in sufficient quantities is available.

❑ There are **no legal or social issues** pertaining to the use of the input data or proposed resulting business actions.

❑ The application truly needs a data mining approach to solve it, and **no simpler solution** is available. As a general rule, if the problem is open to hypothesis, it may well not be a data mining problem. In these cases, simple OLAP, MDA, or relational tools may be sufficient.

For a first-time project, the following criteria could be added:

❏ The scope of the application is limited. Try to show results within weeks rather than months.

❏ The data sources should be limited to those that are well known, relatively clean and, for in-house data, freely accessible.

❏ The number of new skills that are needed is limited. Avoid, where possible, new hardware and software platforms and new data sources.

In-House or Outsource?

As with any technology, there are several ways of getting involved with it—do the work in-house, outsource the work entirely, or set up some hybrid approach. In general, the advantages and disadvantages of the in-house and outsource options are no different for data mining than for general IT.

The attractions of in-house data mining are typically those of in-house developments, namely:

❏ **Skills enhancement**

For organizations that are committed to long-term data mining, doing the work in-house is clearly useful for building the necessary skills. This is especially true for those organizations with an active statistics or mathematical computing department.

❏ **Reduced costs**

Over the long term, the costs of in-house mining are typically less than outsourced contracts.

Nevertheless, given the nature of and current state of the art in data mining, a number of factors favor outsourced contracts, especially for initial projects. These factors are:

❏ **Time to market**

➣ Early adopters of data mining are getting involved for large competitive gain. However, in today's competitive environment, these opportunities are short lived. Time to market is often critical to success.

➣ Product development and life cycles are becoming shorter while customer demands for better choice and quality are increasing. There is less time to develop new products and services, and, when developed and launched, they must break even in a shorter period of time.

> ➤ Consequently, many data mining projects are carried out in reaction mode rather than as the result of a more long-term business strategy.

❏ **High entry costs**

> ➤ Data mining skills are still scarce, and it takes some time and money to acquire them.

> ➤ Although data mining product costs vary, all strong, multitask tools on large platforms are expensive.

> ➤ Hardware costs, especially where SMP and MPP platforms are necessary to guarantee successful data mining, are clearly a major element in the total cost calculation.

❏ **New technology**

> ➤ Because there is not yet a clearly perceived technology leader in data mining, many organizations are postponing their decision to develop in-house solutions and are waiting for the expected shakeout of vendors before they make major purchasing decisions.

> ➤ It is difficult for purchasers to assess and compare the data mining solutions of different vendors in the absence of experience with the technology and the lack of common industry standards.

> ➤ No single data mining tool guarantees a successful approach for all situations for all organizations. Solutions to a business problem typically involve working with several different techniques and/or tools, usually including some traditional visualization and data analysis tools. Getting the right mix of new and traditional technologies is not simple, let alone learning to use the new technology properly.

> ➤ The Internet is allowing a blurring of the distinction between in-house and outsourced projects. It is now possible to mine data over the Internet by using service bureau hardware and consulting services. Equally, consultants can be hired to work at the customer site, using hardware and software that is accessible over the Internet or leased for the duration of the project.

The bottom line here is that there is probably no single right answer to the in-house or outsource question. However, it is probably fair to say that at this time the established data mining consultant groups have a good headstart over the resources that would be available in most in-house situations. Yet, if an organization is to put its business intelligence services on a more strategic footing, data mining skills will have to be developed in-house. This realization by many organizations helps to explain the current popularity of small, proof-of-concept projects where consultants work side-by-side with internal managers and technical professionals.

Assessing Vendor Solutions

The task of assessing any of the increasingly large number of data mining solutions naturally presents a challenge to most in-house development teams who are not familiar with data mining.

"Data Mining Techniques" on page 70 provides an overview of the current state of the art in data mining solutions and "Evaluating Vendor Solutions" on page 89 offers hints and tips when assessing the data mining solutions of vendors.

The task is challenging because:

❑ The data mining technology is relatively new and immature.

❑ There are no widely accepted industry standards for comparison purposes.

❑ The team will be faced with many new and highly specialized data mining vendors (many of whom they have never dealt with before).

Under these circumstances, good general advice is to:

❑ Look for solutions (management consultancy, data mining services, applications, and tools) rather than tools alone. Data mining services and applications help new entrants get a quick startup.

❑ Select a multitask tool that has expert and novice user modes.

❑ Select a vendor who is not necessarily fixed on one specific data mining tool or, indeed, on data mining alone to solve the problem.

Skills and Timescales

Both the requirements for skills and the likely project timescales will vary according to whether you choose in-house or outsourced development.

In many cases the introduction of data mining to an organization may be part of a more general management or business intelligence consultancy engagement where a broad scope of skills will be involved. Here we restrict the discussion to those skills that are necessary to support the actual data mining process itself.

"The Data Mining Process" on page 41 describes the various skills that are needed. Clearly, with an in-house development, the organization itself must provide the skills. Even with outsourced projects, however, there is still a strong requirement for internal skills. Indeed, newcomers to data mining commonly underestimate the level of involvement that management and professionals must have with external service providers.

The data mining team will consist of the:

- Sponsor - influential, focused on business value, enthusiastic
- User group - owners of the business value definition of the project and evaluators of the project's success
- Business analyst - experienced in the domain and application area
- Data analyst - experienced in EDA and data mining
- Data management specialist - experienced in database administration, has access to the physical data (including the relevant metadata)
- The project manager - experienced in project management

Whether the project is developed in-house or is outsourced, the organization itself will still have to provide the sponsor, user group, business analyst, and the data management specialist.

If the role of the data analyst is to be filled from in-house resources, then good recruiting grounds are typically the data analysis group or the advanced technology group. Many large organizations have such groups, which are typically involved in traditional EDA and leading-edge technologies. When looking for new data mining skills, do not be deceived by the increasing ease of use of the newest data mining tools. The real issue here is not so much the use of the tool, but rather the ability of the analyst to prepare the analytical data model and to make good sense of the output.

Timescales will vary according to several general factors not directly related to data mining. These include the project objectives, whether the project is outsourced or carried out in-house, and the level of skills available. Specific data mining considerations that will most influence project time are the accessibility of the data and the complexity of the analytical data model. Accessibility of the data includes the number of data sources and the cleanliness of the selected data.

Timescales will increase with greater numbers of data sources and lower quality data. More complex analytical data models will increase the effort needed to transform the data before mining it.

A good general rule-of-thumb is to try to contain initial, proof-of-concept data mining projects to less than three months. It is critical to be able to quickly demonstrate the validity and benefits of the new technology.

Critical Success Factors

In this section we summarize the key factors that make for a successful data mining project: the right people, the right application, and the right data.

1. Right people (from vision to visualization)
   - A sponsor
   - A user group
   - A consultant or someone who has "been there, done that"
   - A business analyst with domain expertise
   - A data analyst

2. Right application (must be high impact)
   - Clearly understood business objectives
   - A solid cost-benefit analysis
   - A significant impact on business problem or opportunity
   - Achievable in less than three months

3. Right data (remember: garbage in, garbage out)
   - A clean supply of data
   - A limited set of data sources (ideally one—the data warehouse)
   - A solid analytical data model

Some readers may have noticed that data mining technology is absent from our list of critical success factors. Although clearly a solid technology is a critical part of the success story, it probably does not warrant a place among the top three Over time, the technology will begin to become commoditized and slowly disappear into the surrounding applications and technical infrastructure. In the long term, successful data mining is, and will always be, far more about people, business issues, and data than about the underlying technology.

Conclusions

While data mining is still in its infancy, it is business as usual for many progressive organizations today. Although many of the early adopters are industry-leading players, data mining strategies and technology are increasingly filtering down to the smaller organizations. Early reports of successes are encouraging, although success is by no means guaranteed. Data mining is an evolutionary step along the path of problem solving through data analysis, and there is little magic in the approach.

Comparisons between the current stage of data mining and the initial gold rushes of the nineteenth century are often well made. Old miners faced many problems: hugely overpriced equipment, fellow miners eager to hijack mining claims, and, more deadly than any grizzly bear, grossly overstated success stories. All of these threats are still there today—it is just that the grizzly bears are dressed a little differently.

The message is clear. If you *are* starting out on the mining trail, then start now, but start small, and, above all, don't leave base camp without an expert guide!

A

IBM's Data Mining Solution

This appendix is an overview of the IBM data mining solution, which includes data mining tools, applications, and services.

For additional and up-to-date information on any of the components of the solution, contact your IBM marketing representative or consult Appendix C on page 169.

Data Mining Tools

This section features IBM's Intelligent Miner (Version 1, Release 1) and some companion products. We position each of the products within the overall data mining solution and describe them in overviews.

Intelligent Miner

Intelligent Miner is IBM's data mining tool kit. The key distinguishing features of the product are:

❏ A broad selection of mining algorithms, many of which had existed and proven their value before incorporation into the Intelligent Miner product. Many of the algorithms have patented designs.

❏ Interoperability between algorithms, that is, the results of one algorithm may be passed as input to another algorithm

❏ Scalability, supporting large data volumes on all IBM platforms

❏ An application programming interface (API) for custom and vendor application development

❏ A Result API to attach third-party tools for visualization and results analysis

In the rest of this section, we describe the Intelligent Miner in detail, using the template for data mining tool assessment established in "Evaluating Vendor Solutions" on page 89.

Data Mining Process Support

❏ **Data Preparation**

➤ Data Selection

- Flat files

- DB2

- Oracle and Sybase (through a built-in fast import facility)

- Other relational and legacy data sources (through IBM's DataJoinerproduct)

- Data types: numeric, categorical

➤ Data Preprocessing and Transformation

- Aggregate values using SQL column functions such as AVG, SUM, and COUNT

- Calculate new values using SQL expressions

- Case conversion

- Copy and/or sort database records to file for mining

- Discard records with missing values

- Discretize into quantiles

- Discretize into ranges

- Encode missing values
- Encode invalid values
- Filter variables out of input records
- Filter records out of input database
- Get random sample of records in input database
- Group records (through SQL functions and expressions)
- Join relational data sources
- Map input variable values
- Pivot embedded variables structures into separate records

❑ **Data Mining**

The data mining techniques supported are:

➤ Database segmentation, through:

- Demographic clustering
- Neural clustering using theKohonen feature map method

➤ Classification, through:

- Tree induction
- Neural induction (through back propagation neural network)
- Value prediction (through radial basis function)
- Associations discovery
- Sequential pattern discovery
- Similar time sequence discovery

❑ **Analysis of Results and Assimilation of Knowledge**

➤ Specialized results visualization for all algorithms

➤ Export of results to DB2 for resultsvisualization by third-party tools

Technical Considerations

In this section, we present an overview of the architecture of Intelligent Miner and use the architecture as a basis for discussing several technical considerations.

In general, the Intelligent Miner uses a client/server architecture. Data mining is performed on the server. Data definition and interpretation of the results are performed on the client. The API provides an interface to the functions that are accessible from the client, thus triggering the execution of server functions. Figure 46 illustrates the main components of the architecture:

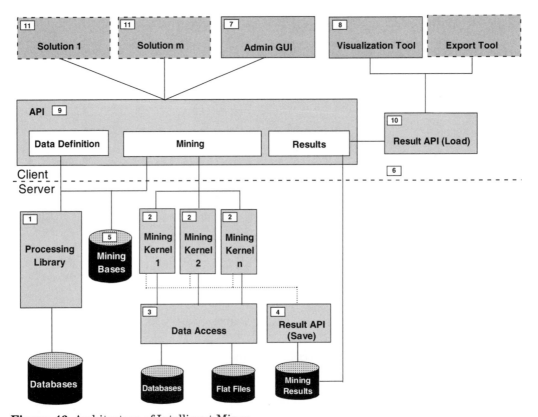

Figure 46. Architecture of Intelligent Miner

1 Processing library: Provides the data preprocessing and transformation functions.

2 Mining kernels: These are—in object technology terminology—essentially classes, or objects, that represent the implementation of each data mining technique.

3 Data access: Provides read and write access to both flat files and relational tables. (This service is available only to toolkit internal functions, not applications.)

4 Result API: Enables exporting of mining results. On the server side, the kernels write the results files. On the client side, the results can be loaded for visualization and used by other applications.

5 Mining bases: These are essentially repositories that hold information about the input data, the mining run settings, and the corresponding mining results. They contain the metadata for the mining runs.

6 Client/server interface: Shown as a dashed line, this component addresses the communication between the client layer and the server layer. It is implemented using remote procedure calls (RPCs).

7 Administration graphical user interface (GUI): Provides user control functions for specifying parameters and settings for the mining techniques and data processing functions. Through this GUI the user can also manage the mining results, that is, browse, save new results, or delete previously saved results.

8 Visualization tool: Provides several specialized visualizers for the display of the mining results.

9 API: Provides user function to control the behavior of the data mining kernels and data processing functions from outside the GUI. The Environment Layer API provides an interface to the functions that are accessible from the client, thus triggering the execution of server functions.

10 Result API: Provides on the client side a set of C++ classes as the basis for writing data export routines to other software products. For instance, the Result API for association rules and sequential patterns provides functions for retrieving association rules, large item sets, and sequential patterns from the exported result files.

11 Solution 1...m: Examples of custom and vendor applications that can be developed on top of the API functions.

The Intelligent Miner architecture provides an environment that supports openness, integration, scalability, and performance in the ways described below:

❑ **Openness**

➤ Result API

➤ Server availability on the most important IBM server platforms

➤ Client availability on IBM and non-IBM platforms

❑ **Scalability**

➤ Patented algorithms, designed for large data volumes

➤ Client/server architecture

➤ Server availability on IBM's MPP platform, with linear scalability in data access through DB2 Parallel Edition

❏ **Performance**

➤ Server availability on all IBM platforms (including IBM's MPP platform)

➤ Patented algorithms

Intelligent Miner User Scenario

In this scenario the user interacts with Intelligent Miner to solve a common business problem—database segmentation. The objective is to segment a fictitious file of motor insurance claims into several homogeneous sub-populations and analyze the profiles of the claimants in the segments.

For clarity, we omit some of the details of the data mining process. For example, the time-consuming data preparation step is largely missing. Thus, this scenario is a very simplified view of a real-life data mining process. Do not be tricked by the apparent ease with which data mining tools can be used—real data mining is never this simple.

Figure 47 is an overview of the scenario, which consists of four main steps:

1 Specify Input/Output Data - Define the data to be mined, in this case, the insurance claims file.

2 Process Data - Preprocess the input data, in this case, to handle missing values.

3 Select Technique - Select the appropriate data mining technique, in this case, segmentation.

4 Work on Results - Select visualization tools to analyze the results, in this case, specialized tools to display and drill down on the customer segments.

Figure 48 shows the main Intelligent Miner window. The window shows several controls that reflect the steps in the data mining process.

***Step.* 1** Specify Input/Output Data

The user starts by clicking on **Specify Input/Output Data**, and the Specifying the Data Source/Target-Files window appears (Figure 49).

The objective of this step is to select the input file and define its variables. (For database input, the details of the variables are retrieved automatically from the database catalogs.) The **Browse** push button

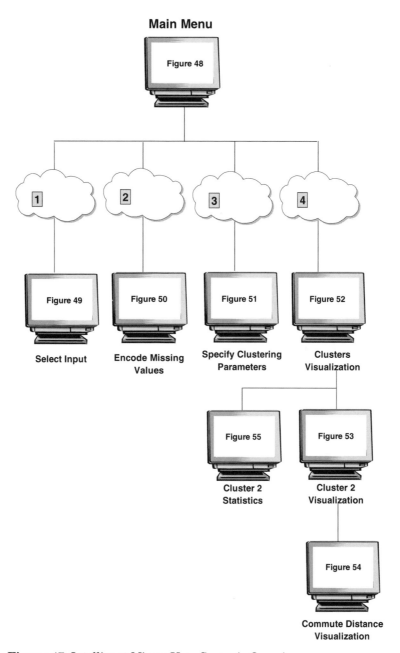

Figure 47. Intelligent Miner: User Scenario Overview

Figure 48. Intelligent Miner: Main Window

Figure 49. Specifying the Data Source/Target - Files

allows the user to visually inspect the content of the input file. This inspection is often done by analysts just to visually confirm the general layout and content of the input data.

After defining the variables the user clicks on the **OK** push button and the Intelligent Miner - Main Window reappears. The user then clicks **Process Data**, and the Process Data window appears (Figure 50).

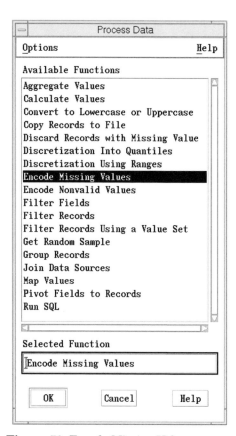

Figure 50. Encode Missing Values

Step. **2** Process Data

During the visual inspection of the input data in Step 1, the user may have noticed that some important variables were not recorded in certain cases. For example, perhaps the number of claims is missing in cases where the claimant has recently transferred into the company. In any event, the objective here is to correct this situation. A typical solution is to encode the variable with some average or typical value.

In this case the user decides to encode the missing claims variable values with zero. In fact, Intelligent Miner will place the new zero value in a newly created variable so that both old and new values are available for inspection during analysis of the mining results.

The user clicks on the **OK** push button, returns to the Intelligent Miner - Main Window, and then clicks **Select Technique** followed by **Clustering**. The Intelligent Miner - Clustering window appears (Figure 51).

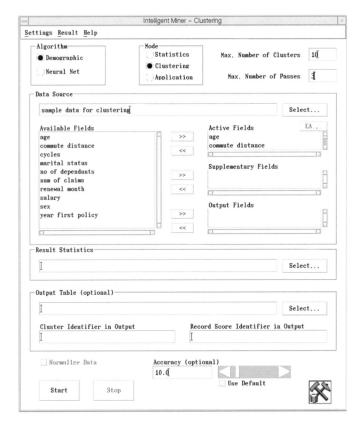

Figure 51. Intelligent Miner: Clustering Window

Step. 3 Select Technique

The objective of this step is to select the appropriate data mining algorithm and specify the variables to be used for mining along with some mining control parameters.

In this case the user selects demographic segmentation (called *clustering* in Intelligent Miner) because of the presence of several categorical variables, such as marital status and sex. From the list of available variables (called *fields* in Intelligent Miner), the user can select variables as active (for use in the segmentation) and supplementary (not for use in the segmentation but carried to the output file to assist in the post-mining analysis).

For both the demographic and neural net segmentation algorithms it is possible to select three operational modes:

1. Statistics - Calculate statistics such as mode, mean, and standard deviation for numeric variables, both active and supplementary; do not do any segmentation.
2. Clustering - Segment the input data file using the active variables.
3. Application - Segment the input file on the basis of the segmentation information created during a previous mining run that used the same data format, for example, to assign a small number of new customer records to existing segments.

In this case, the user selects **Clustering**.

Several mining control parameters are available to the user. One of these parameters is the maximum number of segments that will be developed by the algorithm during the segmentation. Specifying a small number of segments will improve performance but limit the homogeneity of the segments and the accuracy of the overall solution. Specifying a high number of segments may produce too diverse a spread of segments and, of course, will take longer to run. The maximum number of segments is optional. If a number is not specified, the algorithm automatically determines the optimal number on the basis of the other control parameters discussed below. In this case, the user sets the maximum number of segments to 10.

Another control parameter is the maximum number of passes over the input data that the algorithm should make. Limiting the number of passes reduces the processing time required to perform a segmentation, but it also reduces the accuracy. Equally, specifying multiple passes through the data improves the quality of the generated segments but at the cost of performance. Usually, two or three passes are recommended to establish a compromise between performance and accuracy. In this case the user specifies 3 passes.

Finally, the accuracy control parameter represents the percentage improvement in segmentation on each pass of the input data. The accuracy value specified is used as a stopping condition such that, if the actual improvement is less than the value specified, no more passes occur. The smaller the value, the more accurate is the segmentation. The user in this case sets the value to 10.0%. The user then clicks the **Start** push button to initiate the mining run. The run terminates when it meets one of the stopping conditions and then displays the segmentation results (Figure 52).

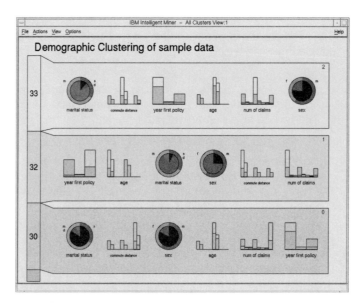

Figure 52. Three Largest Segments

Step. 4 Work on Results

The objective of this step is clearly to analyze the segmentation results.

Figure 52 shows the three largest segments (the other smaller segments have been removed from view); the numbers on the left represent the percentage of records in each segment. Within each segment, the active variables are arranged from left to right in order of decreasing significance. For example, in the case of the second largest segment, the variables *year first policy* and *age* are clearly the most significant. Each variable is depicted by a sub-chart, either a histogram for numeric variables or a pie-chart in the case of categorical variables.

The sub-charts have a special overlay structure that enables them to depict the distribution of the associated variable within both the individual segment and, for comparison purposes, the overall population. To judge the significance of each variable, the user compares the sizes of the corresponding variable distributions for the segment with the size for the overall population. The more the two distributions differ, the more significant is the variable.

The user decides to zoom in on the largest segment (with 33% of the records). The results are displayed in Figure 53.

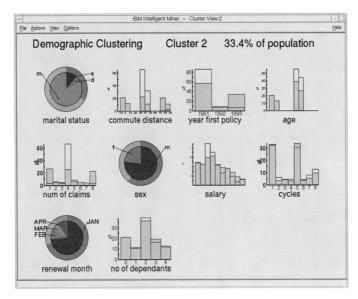

Figure 53. Zoom-In on Largest Segment (33%)

Note that Figure 53 includes all of the active variables (and supplementary variables if there were any) to assist in better understanding the detailed characteristics of the segment. The user can see that the members of this segment are more likely to be older, married men, with mature policies on which they are more likely to have an average number of claims.

The user is surprised by the significance of the *commute distance* variable and decides to take a closer look at the distribution of the variable. The results are shown in Figure 54 on page 154.

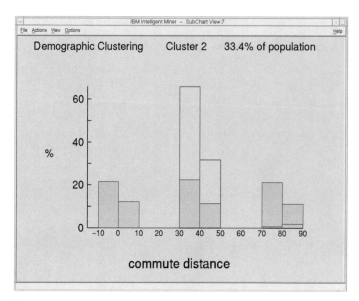

Figure 54. Zoom-In on Commute Distance

Figure 54 illustrates the overlay feature for histograms. The distribution of the *commute distance* variable in the overall population is shown in the darker shading and the distribution within the segment is shown by a dotted outline.

Interpreting the results of the zoom-in, the user observes that the significance of the *commute distance* variable in this segment comes from the highly different pattern of travel of these claimants. It appears that members of this segment are significantly more likely to commute between 30 and 50 miles from home to work than the overall population.

The user has the option of examining statistical details for either all segments, an individual segment, or a sub-chart. Figure 55 on page 155 shows detailed statistics for the largest segment.

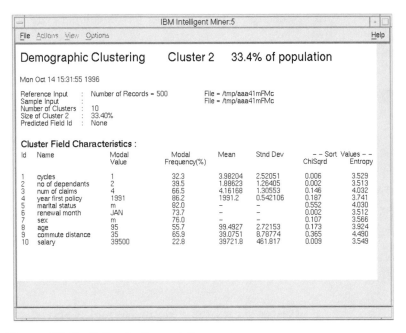

Figure 55. Statistics for Largest Segment

Companion Products

Intelligent Decision Server

IBM Intelligent Decision Server (IDS) is a network computing decision support application server that provides facilities for query and reporting, OLAP, and MDA as well as statistical functions such as regression and time series analysis. (IDS is a derivative of the IBM Data Interpretation System (DIS).) Client interfaces for IDS include the World Wide Web, Lotus Notes, PowerBuilder, and Visual Basic applications; data access from third-party tools is provided through an ODBC interface.

IDS provides decision support with a three-tier architecture (client, application server, database server). Both types of decision-support tools may be appropriate and are complementary.

All IDS analytics are executed on the server and are multithreaded. A key architectural component is the IDS Capsule, effectively a macro of data access and analysis tasks (called *IDS transformers*) that can be linked together through a visual programming interface into a sharable decision support function (see Figure 56). IDS comes with a library of prewritten Capsules but developers are free to create their own.

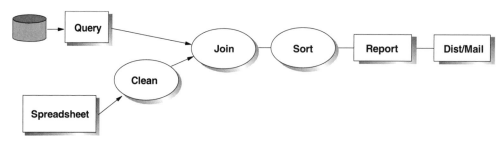

Figure 56. IDS: the Capsule Concept

The IDS Capsule in Figure 56:

❑ Accesses data from a database and a spreadsheet (cleaning the records from the spreadsheet by removing header information)
❑ Joins the two data streams
❑ Sorts the date into ascending order
❑ Produces a report
❑ Distributes the report through a mailing list

IDS developers use IDS transformers to add value to the Capsule processing. Transformers cover a wide range of functions, from data cleaning, to data manipulation, to statistical analysis.

Integration with IBM Intelligent Miner: Figure 57 on page 157 depicts the integration of IDS with IBM Intelligent Miner. The IDS Capsule and transformer technology is used to integrate the two products. IDS provides transformers that access functions provided by Intelligent Miner, thus allowing for the development of decision support applications based on advanced data mining analytics.

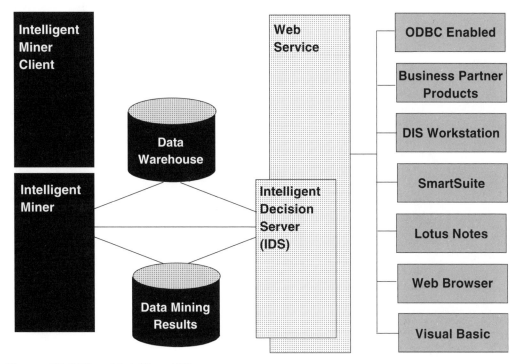

Figure 57. IDS and Intelligent Miner

Visual Warehouse

Visual Warehouse is IBM's data warehousing fast-startup offering. The product builds and maintains scalable, accessible data marts with substantially reduced costs, timescales, and skills when compared with traditional data warehousing approaches.

Data marts can be sourced from many popular relational and nonrelational databases. Relational sources include all DB2 family members (whether running on IBM or non-IBM platforms such as Microsoft NT), Oracle, Informix, Sybase, Microsoft SQL Server or any ODBC compliant database. Some nonrelational sources are IMS on MVS, VSAM files on MVS, and flat files on LAN, VM, and MVS.

Data marts can be built on most DB2 Family databases (whether running on IBM or non-IBM platforms).

Client access is supported from most popular workstation platforms such as Windows (3.1 and 3.11, 95, and NT), Macintosh, AIX, OS/400, OS/2, HP-UX, and Solaris.

The key design points for IBM Visual Warehouse are end-to-end support for the warehousing process, and a strong, scalable architecture.

End-to-End Support

Visual Warehouse provides facilities to define, build, manage, monitor, and maintain data marts. The contents of the data mart are defined in terms of business data views and processes, which can then be inter-linked and built into what is effectively an integrated data model and process model of the data mart's business subject area. Once built, the model doubles as a data mart management mechanism, controlling the accessing, loading, and processing of the data within the data mart. Monitoring and administration facilities help the data mart administrator see in-flight the status of the process flows within the data mart and maintain both data and process controls.

These support facilities are based on several key elements:

Business Views. Similar to database views, business views are images of the data that can be used individually, or in a composite, to reflect actual business processes. Business views are the fundamental building blocks of Visual Warehouse. Each business view has attributes that define its operation, information content, and interaction with other business views. The business view is externalized in the form of one or more persistent and/or transient relational tables. A persistent table is one that permanently exists, whereas a transient table exists only until the business view process completes.

Data mart process monitors. Visual Warehouse provides facilities to monitor and control the data mart processes. For example, the administration client can monitor data mart activity, view logs, and maintain security and authorizations, or a report could be created with such information as the average time it takes each day, week, or month to refresh the target databases, the trends in data volume growth, or the number of unsuccessful data loads.

Editions. When a business view is defined to Visual Warehouse, a key attribute is the number of editions that will be kept. When a business view is refreshed, the new data content is referred to as a new *edition*. Editions of business views represent the history of the informational data. For example, the data may be saved by time periods, such as daily, weekly, monthly, and quarterly editions. The management of editions is automatically performed by Visual Warehouse. Editions provide the ability to store history data for trend analysis and period-to-period comparisons. Visual Warehouse supports an unlimited number of editions for a business view.

Schedules. Visual Warehouse provides scheduling facilities to automate the execution of business views that refresh the data in the data mart. Execution can be scheduled on demand, at a specified time, or on a repeating time interval. Multi-level schedules can also be defined for each business view. The combination of scheduling, triggers, and cascaded business views provides a powerful data mart operational environment.

Versions. Versions represent different definitions of a particular business view and provide a structured data mart change management process. They provide the capability to modify, update, or otherwise change a business view definition while still maintaining the original definition, thus enabling a managed transition to a new version, the use of multiple versions concurrently, or the creation of a version history for audit purposes.

Cascading Business Views. Execution of one business view can automatically cause the execution of other business views. This process is called *cascading*. A cascaded business view can execute at the same time as the originating business view, or it can execute after the originating business view completes. Visual Warehouse supports conditional execution of cascaded business views with the use of triggers.

Triggers. A trigger is a user-defined program (UDP) that can be used to perform post-processing for a business view. For example, an e-mail notification could be sent on completion of the execution of a particular business view. This would signal to the business client that a new edition of the data is available. Triggers are a powerful technique for revealing information that might otherwise have gone unnoticed to users and data mart administrators.

User-Defined Programs. Visual Warehouse supports UDPs to transform and manipulate source data with capabilities beyond those of standard SQL. For example, a UDP could be used for data cleansing, data enhancement, reconciliation, notification, or transformations that require complex programming logic. A UDP can be any program that can run as an executable file.

Strong, Scalable Architecture

The Visual Warehouse architecture is built around the following key components:

The Warehouse Manager. This component controls the interaction of various data mart components and automates data mart processes through a scheduling facility.

The Control Database. This database holds the control information used by the Warehouse Manager and includes business views, schedules, operational logs, and associated metadata.

Administration Clients. These clients provide the interface to the Visual Warehouse operations functions. These functions include defining business views, registering data sources, fingering source data, defining data mart target tables, managing security, determining data refresh schedules, and monitoring the execution of data mart processes.

Agents. Agents handle the accessing of source data and its filtering, transformation, subsetting, and delivery to the data mart. Agents can be placed on different platforms to better distribute the data processing load across the network.

Parallel Visual Explorer

IBM Parallel Visual Explorer is a high-resolution visualization and data analysis tool, specifically developed for very large data sets that contain multidimensional data. It is attractive to users of traditional statistical processing who need a rapid, accurate tool to identify hypotheses and a convenient method of communicating analysis results to their customers, a business manager, or a client.

IBM Parallel Visual Explorer is based on a methodology of parallel (as opposed to traditional, perpendicular) coordinates that provides the only known approach of displaying unambiguous relationships between and among many variables in very large data sets, without loss of information.

Diamond

Diamond is a highly interactive graphical visualization toolkit for exploring relationships between variables in multivariate data. The basic philosophy of Diamond is to depict data and statistics with pictures and let the user manipulate these pictures to gain insight into the underlying patterns. Diamond provides many simultaneous data presentations, including various 2-D, 3-D, and higher dimensionality plots. In this sense, Diamond is a graphical spreadsheet for data mining, an interactive tool for running "what-if" experiments in real time. It can be used as a stand-alone data analysis tool or in conjunction with other analytical tools for data mining, modeling, and analysis.

Visualization Data Explorer

IBM Visualization Data Explorer is a third-generation visualization application and toolkit. It includes a full set of tools for manipulating, transforming, processing, realizing, rendering, and animating data. Visualization and analysis can be based on several methods, including points, lines, areas, volumes, images or geometric primitives in any combination. A developers toolkit includes Data Explorer's visual program editor (VPE).

Figure 30 is an example of Visualization Data Explorer output.

Data Mining Applications

Generic Applications

Business Discovery Solutions

Business discovery solutions address several common business objectives in the related areas of CRM and database marketing. Two solutions are offered:

- ❑ **Customer Discovery**, a suite of components for use in CRM and database marketing applications. The suite includes components for data fusion (database creation from disparate sources), response scoring (predictive modeling of customer purchasing patterns, attrition analysis, and so on), profit scoring (customer profitability analysis), campaign management (control of marketing programs and channels), and POS marketing (distribution of messages to POS terminals such as automatic teller machines (ATMs).

- ❑ **Product Discovery**, an application for what is most commonly known as MBA. MBA aims to discover shoppers' purchasing patterns by revealing subsets of purchased items and the affinities among the subsets.

Industry-Specific Applications

Most of IBM's Industry Solution Units (ISUs) offer data mining solutions. Naturally, the format and level of maturity of these solutions vary from ISU to ISU. Currently, formal data mining solutions have been announced by the ISUs for banking, telecommunications, healthcare, and distribution.

Banking, Finance and Securities

FinanceQuery. This solution, designed specifically for the finance industry, includes several classic data mining applications and is offered as a turnkey solution.

The applications include customer behavior modeling (individual scoring for propensity to buy and retain products); profitability analysis (profitability for an individual officer, branch, product, product group, and so on, along with "what if" capabilities); marketing campaign management (monitoring marketing programs and channels); and customer data analysis (customer segmentation profiling). The solution is offered with a set of services including planning, implementation, and education.

Telecommunications and Media

DecisionEdge. This offering is aimed at building an entire business intelligence environment for telecommunications organizations and includes hardware, software, and services.

The offering is built around a core system and suites of packaged and custom applications. The core system includes the server, relational database, market reporting tool, telecommunications marketing data model, and implementation services. The packaged applications, which are customizable, cover critical industry applications such as response scoring, marketing campaign management, profitability analysis, and customer segmentation. The custom applications are aimed at providing individual client organizations with unique, breakthrough applications based on technologies from data mining and/or OLAP.

Healthcare

The Fraud and Abuse Management System (FAMS). This application tackles a critical problem in the healthcare industry: fraud and abusive practice by healthcare providers.

FAMS focuses on assisting health insurance organizations in all key aspects of dealing with fraud and abuse: detection, investigation, settlement, and prevention of recurrence. It features peer group profiling, ranking of individual providers, investigative and charting tools, and tools for ongoing monitoring of deviant behavior.

FAMS was designed with input from healthcare and fraud detection specialists and is based on expert system technology.

Distribution

RetailQuery. This solution for the distribution and retail industries consists of two specialized suites of applications:

❑ **Target** includes data analysis and reporting, cross-selling analysis, and electronic marketing.

❏ **Plan-It** includes development and management of merchandise and allocation plans.

Data Mining Services

Consultancy Services

Consultancy services address data mining in the overall context of business intelligence. The objective is to ensure rapid startup with a high probability of quick ROI by combining industry knowledge with data mining expertise.

Worldwide, IBM has a team of some 18,000 industry specialists. Those specialists who have data mining expertise in addition to their industry knowledge tend to be concentrated in certain industries, namely, banking, insurance, telecommunications, retail, and healthcare.

Although each consultancy engagement will vary, a typical engagement has the following tasks and deliverables:

❏ Analysis of the client's business environment to assess the appropriateness of a data mining solution

❏ Selection of one of more good candidate data mining projects

❏ Definition of the business objectives of the projects, including preparation of the business case

❏ Recommendation of a solution, including systems architecture and user tools selection

❏ Project plan, including timescales, resources, and risks

Implementation Services

Implementation services are focused on the implementation of a specific data mining project. IBM provides both in-house and outsourced services in this area. In-house services typically involve provision and integration of several components of the overall data mining solution including hardware, software, and data mining tools and applications. Solutions may include generic or industry-specific applications. Both IBM and non-IBM platforms and software are supported. Where appropriate, IBM's business partners are used for specialized components and services.

Outsourced implementation services provide off-site data mining and preparation of results.

Education Services

IBM offers several education services, ranging from high-level executive conferences to hands-on technical workshops. Here are some examples:

☐ **Intelligent Miner Workshop**: detailed, four-day, hands-on workshop with the Intelligent Miner product for data analysts

☐ **Data Mining Customer Workshop**: intense, five-day, exploration of data mining business and technical aspects for business and data analysts

☐ **Themed Executive Conferences**: One- or two-day executive conferences focused on data mining solutions within a specific industry or business area.

Related Services

IBM offers several education and implementation services in the related area of data warehousing. Some examples are:

☐ **Data Warehouse Consultancy and Implementation Services**

> ➤ Data Warehouse Strategy and Architecture (business case, technical systems and data architecture, implementation strategy, initial project selection)

> ➤ Data Warehouse Solution Design (modeling, data mapping, end-user interface, hardware and software installation)

> ➤ Data Warehouse Project Management (coordination, resource planning and allocation, user training)

☐ **Data Warehouse Education Services**

> ➤ Visual Warehouse Overview (one day)

> ➤ Visual Warehouse Implementation Workshop (three days, hands-on)

> ➤ Data Warehouse Enablement: Methods and Techniques (three days)

Emerging Technologies

Text and Media Mining

IBM's text mining solution is a set of technologies, such as linguistic analysis, mathematical data analysis, and graphical navigation techniques, that help users manage large amounts of textual data. The solution includes:

IBM Text Navigator

IBM Text Navigator summarizes large numbers of documents, for example, newspaper articles, into a single map or virtual library. The tool can completely and automatically cluster documents according to their contents. Each cluster contains documents that are conceptually similar, in other words, that deal with related topics.

IBM Technology Watch

IBM Technology Watch is aimed at helping strategic decision-making in companies as well as research and defense organizations. Specifically, it analyzes international patent databases and online technical and research publications in such fields as chemistry, pharmacy, aeronautics, physics, and engineering. Technology Watch automatically classifies the documents by content into clusters.

MediaMiner

MediaMiner is a collection of beta technologies that applies mining and advanced search and retrieval techniques to text, audio, image, and video data. The function is focused on:

❑ **Text search and retrieval**: full-text search with Boolean, proximity, and masking operations; summarization and classification of documents by content; indexing of documents; document content statistics.

❑ **Text Mining**: linguistic analysis of documents to identify key elements across documents for indexing and for use by retrieval algorithms; clustering of documents by title and content; navigation through document clusters.

❑ **Image Mining**: indexing and ranking of images by image content (color, texture, layout); querying of images by image content; querying of images by conceptual queries such as "forest scene," "ice," or "cylinder."

Internet Mining

Surf-Aid

The Surf-Aid application is aimed at improving the development and management of Internet marketing strategies. It applies data mining algorithms to Web access logs for marketing-related pages. Analysis of the click streams of the site visitors helps to discover customer preferences and behavior patterns. The results can be used for analyzing the effectiveness of marketing materials, improving general Web site organization, and designing better Web materials such as pages that are dynamically configured according to a visitor's previous click stream or observed preferences.

Miscelleanous

Advanced Scout

IBM Advanced Scout is an application for assisting coaches and officials of the U.S. National Basketball Association (NBA). It works by applying data mining techniques to game statistics, for example, shots blocked, assists made, and personal fouls. The statistics are gathered during play and are tied to the time-stamped video footage of the game for easy post-game review and analysis. Basketball is a very fast-moving game, and Advanced Scout detects significant patterns of play that may otherwise escape the attention of coaches and officials. Post-game analysis helps coaches develop better winning strategies. Advanced Scout is used increasingly by NBA teams such as the New York Knicks and Miami Heat.

B

Special Notices

The information in this publication is not intended as the specification of any programming interfaces that are provided by Intelligent Miner, Intelligent Decision Server, Visual Warehouse, Parallel Visual Explorer, Diamond, and Visualization Data Explorer. See the PUBLICATIONS section of the IBM Programming Announcement for these products for more information about what publications are considered to be product documentation.

References in this publication to IBM products, programs or services do not imply that IBM intends to make these available in all countries in which IBM operates. Any reference to an IBM product, program, or service is not intended to state or imply that only IBM's product, program, or service may be used. Any functionally equivalent program that does not infringe any of IBM's intellectual property rights may be used instead of the IBM product, program or service.

Information in this book was developed in conjunction with use of the equipment specified, and is limited in application to those specific hardware and software products and levels.

IBM may have patents or pending patent applications covering subject matter in this document. The furnishing of this document does not give you any license to these patents. You can send license inquiries, in writing, to the IBM Director of Licensing, IBM Corporation, 500 Columbus Avenue, Thornwood, NY 10594 USA.

The information contained in this document has not been submitted to any formal IBM test and is distributed AS IS. The information about non-IBM ("vendor") products in this book has been supplied by the vendor and IBM assumes no responsibility for its accuracy or completeness. The use of this information or the implementation of any of these techniques is a customer responsibility and depends on the customer's ability to evaluate and integrate them into the customer's operational environment. While each item may have been reviewed by IBM for accuracy in a specific situation, there is no guarantee that the same or similar results will be obtained elsewhere. Customers attempting to adapt these techniques to their own environments do so at their own risk.

The following terms are trademarks of the International Business Machines Corporation in the United States and/or other countries:

AIX	C Set ++
DB2	IBM
IMS	

The following terms are trademarks of other companies:

UNIX is a registered trademark in the United States and other countries licensed exclusively through X/Open Company Limited.

Microsoft, Windows, and the Windows 95 logo are trademarks or registered trademarks of Microsoft Corporation.

Other trademarks are trademarks of their respective companies.

C

Further Reading and Resources

This bibliography lists books, articles, and Internet resources for further reading on the topics of data mining and data warehousing.

Most of the books and articles have been selected as a logical next step for readers of this book and do not require an in-depth technical knowledge.

Books

Adriaans P., D. Zantinge, 1996, *Data Mining*, Harlow England: Addison-Wesley.

Bigus J., 1996, *Data Mining with Neural Networks*, New York, NY: McGraw-Hill.

Communications of the ACM, 1996, *Special Edition on Data Mining* Communications of the ACM, Nov. 1996.

Devlin B., 1996, *Data Warehouse, from Architecture to Implementation*, Reading MA: Addison-Wesley.

Donadio S., 1992, *New York Public Library Book of Twentieth Century American Quotations*, Warner Brothers.

Gardner, C., 1996, *IBM Data Mining Technology*, http://booksrv2.raleigh.ibm.com/cgi-bin/bookmgr/bookmgr.cmd/BOOKS/datamine/

Gill H., P. Rao, 1996, *The Official Guide to Data Warehousing*, Indianapolis, IN: Que Corporation.

Graham, S, 1996, *The Foundations of Wisdom: A Study of the Financial Impacts of Data Warehousing*, Toronto, Ontario: International Data Corporation (IDC)

IBM, 1996, *Intelligent Miner User Guide, Version 1 Release 1*, SH12-6213-00

Inmon, W. H., 1992, *Building the Data Warehouse*, Wellesley, MA: QED Technical Publishing Group

Jubak, J., 1992, *In the Image of the Brain: Breaking the Barrier between the Human Mind and Intelligent Machines*, Boston: Little, Brown.

McClean S., B. Scotnay, 1996, *The Data Mining Report*, Uxbridge, UK: UNICOM Seminars Ltd.

Parsaye K., M. Chignell, 1993, *Intelligent Database Tools & Applications*, New York, NY: John Wiley & Sons, Inc.

Peppers D., M. Rogers, 1993, *The One to One Future, Building Relationships One Customer at a Time*, New York, NY: Currency Doubleday.

Rich E., K. Knight, 1991, *Artificial Intelligence*, New York, NY: McGraw-Hill.

Rumelhart D. E., J. L. McClelland, 1986, *Parallel Distributed Processing: Explorations in the Microstructure of Cognition*, Cambridge, MA: MIT Press.

Two Crows Corporation, 1997, *Data Mining: Products and Markets*, Potomac, MD: Two Crows Corporation.

Weiss S., C. Kulikowski, 1991, *Computer Systems That Learn: Classification and Prediction Methods from Statistics, Neural Nets, Machine Learning and Expert Systems*, Redwood City, CA: Morgan Kaufmann.

Articles

Arning, A, R. Agrawal, P. Raghavan, 1996, A Linear Method for Deviation Detection in Large Databases, *Proceedings of the Second International Conference on Knowledge Discovery & Data Mining*, Menlo Park, CA: The AAAI Press / The MIT Press, p. 164

Berry, J. et al., 1994, Database Marketing: a Potent New Tool for Selling, *Business Week*, September 5, p. 56

Bort, J., 1996, Data Mining's Midas Touch, *Infoworld*, April 29, p. 7

Brachman, R., T. Anand, 1996, The Process of Knowledge Discovery in Databases: A Human-Centered Approach, *Advances in Knowledge Discovery and Data Mining*, Menlo Park, CA: The AAAI Press / The MIT Press, p. 37

Comaford, C., 1997, Unearthing Data Mining Myths, *PC Week*, January 6

DePomps, B., 1996, Wal-Mart Orders a Super Warehouse, *Information Week*, March 11

Fayyad U., G. Piatetsky-Shapiro, P. Smyth, 1996, Knowledge Discovery and Data Mining: Towards a Unifying Framework, *Proceedings of the Second International Conference on Knowledge Discovery & Data Mining*, Menlo Park, CA: The AAAI Press / The MIT Press, p. 82

Fayyad U., G. Piatetsky-Shapiro, P. Smyth, 1996, From Data Mining to Knowledge Discovery: An Overview, *Advances in Knowledge Discovery and Data Mining*, Menlo Park, CA: The AAAI Press / The MIT Press, p. 1

Howarth, B., 1996, HIC Strikes a Data Mother Lode, *Computerworld*, May 10

Kuntz, M., 1995, Reinventing the Store, *Business Week*, November 27, p. 84

Langley P., H. Simon, 1995, *Applications of Machine Learning and Rule Induction*, Communications of the ACM, November

McMath, R., 1997, Copycat Cupcakes Don't Cut It, *American Demographics*, January, p. 60

Nearhos, J., M. Rothman, M. Viveros, 1996, Applying Data Mining Techniques to a Health Insurance Information System, *Proceedings of the 22nd VLDB Conference*, Bombay, India. By kind permission of the Very Large Database Endowment.

O'Leary, D., 1995, Some Privacy Issues in Knowledge Discovery: The OECD Personal Privacy Guidelines, *IEEE Expert - Intelligent Systems and Their Application*, April, p. 48

Piatetsky-Shapiro G., 1996, Data Mining and Knowledge Discovery Internet Resources, *Advances in Knowledge Discovery and Data Mining*, Menlo Park, CA: The AAAI Press / The MIT Press, p. 593

Piatetsky-Shapiro G. et al., 1996, An Overview of Issues in Developing Industrial Data Mining and Knowledge Discovery Applications, *Proceedings of the Second International Conference on Knowledge Discovery & Data Mining*, Menlo Park, CA: The AAAI Press / The MIT Press, p. 89

Ross, J., 1996, New Rule-Based Systems Tackle Employee Shrink, *Stores*, August, p. 71

Seshadri, V., S. Sasisekharan, S. Weiss, 1996, Data Mining and Forecasting in Large-Scale Telecommunication Networks, *IEEE Expert - Intelligent Systems and Their Application*, February, p. 36

Simoudis, E., 1996, Reality Check for Data Mining, *IEEE Expert - Intelligent Systems and Their Application*, October, p. 26

Simoudis, E. et al., 1995, Developing Customer Vulnerability Models Using Data Mining Techniques, *Proceedings of the International Symposium on Intelligent Data Analysis*, August, Baden-Baden, Germany

Speer, T., 1996, Credit-Card Mania, *American Demographics*, December, p. 30

Spiegler, M., 1996, Marketing Street Culture, Bringing Hip-Hop to the Mainstream, *American Demographics*, November, p. 28

Stoneman, B., 1997, Banking On Customers, *American Demographics*, February, p. 36

Totton, K, 1996, Case Study 2: Telephony Fraud Investigation, *The Data Mining Report*, UNICOM Seminars Ltd., p. 5-6.

Uthurusamy, R., 1996, *From Data Mining to Knowledge Discovery: Current Challenges and Future Directions* in *Advances in Knowledge Discovery and Data Mining*, Menlo Park, CA: The AAAI Press / The MIT Press, p. 561

Verity, W., 1996, A Trillion-Byte Weapon: Marketers Use Massive Computer Power to Woo Customers, *Business Week*, July 31, p. 80

Zanasi A., 1995, Data Mining and Competitive Intelligence through Internet, *Proceedings of the Third Network Information Retrieval Conference*, Milan, Italy: CILEA.

Zanasi A., 1997, Competitive Intelligence through Data Mining Public Sources, *Competitive Intelligence Review*, New York, NY: John Wiley & Sons, Inc.

Internet Resources

The vendor-sponsored sites are those owned by the vendors that are mentioned in this book. The vendor-independent sites have typically been built by private individuals and are currently among the most informative and best-maintained sites on data mining and related topics.

Vendor-Sponsored Sites

DataMind

http://www.datamindcorp.com

HNC Software

http://www.hnc.com/prodsmkt.htm

IBM

http://direct.boulder.ibm.com/bi/
http://www.software.ibm.com/data/products

Integral Solutions Ltd.

http://www.isl.co.uk

Right Information Systems

http://www.4thought.com

SAS Institute Inc.

http://www.sas.com/feature/4qpdm/intro.html

Silicon Graphics

http://www.sgi.com

Vendor-Independent Sites

The Knowledge Discovery Mine

`http://info.gte.com/~kdd/`

The Data Mine

`http://www.cs.bham.ac.uk/~anp/TheDataMine.html`

Companies in Data Mining and Knowledge Discovery

`http://info.gte.com/~kdd/companies.html`

International Conference on Knowledge Discovery and Data Mining

`http://www-aig.jpl.nasa.gov/kddxx`, where xx is 96, 97, and so on

ITSO Publications

For information on ordering these ITSO publications see "How to Get ITSO Redbooks" on page 175.

Redbooks on CD-ROMs

Redbooks are also available on CD-ROMs. **Order a subscription** and receive updates 2-4 times a year at significant savings.

CD-ROM Title	Subscription Number	Collection Kit Number
System/390 Redbooks Collection	SBOF-7201	SK2T-2177
Networking and Systems Management Redbooks Collection	SBOF-7370	SK2T-6022
Transaction Processing and Data Management Redbook	SBOF-7240	SK2T-8038

CD-ROM Title	Subscription Number	Collection Kit Number
AS/400 Redbooks Collection	SBOF-7270	SK2T-2849
RS/6000 Redbooks Collection (HTML, BkMgr)	SBOF-7230	SK2T-8040
RS/6000 Redbooks Collection (PostScript)	SBOF-7205	SK2T-8041
Application Development Redbooks Collection	SBOF-7290	SK2T-8037
Personal Systems Redbooks Collection	SBOF-7250	SK2T-8042

How to Get ITSO Redbooks

This section explains how both customers and IBM employees can find out about ITSO redbooks, CD-ROMs, workshops, and residencies. A form for ordering books and CD-ROMs is also provided.

This information was current at the time of publication, but is continually subject to change. The latest information may be found at URL http://www.redbooks.ibm.com.

How IBM Employees Can Get ITSO Redbooks

Employees may request ITSO deliverables (redbooks, BookManager BOOKs, and CD-ROMs) and information about redbooks, workshops, and residencies in the following ways:

- ❏ **PUBORDER** — to order hardcopies in United States
- ❏ **GOPHER link to the Internet** - type

```
GOPHER.WTSCPOK.ITSO.IBM.COM
```

❏ **Tools disks**

To get LIST3820s of redbooks, type one of the following commands:

```
TOOLS SENDTO EHONE4 TOOLS2 REDPRINT GET SG24xxxx PACKAGE
TOOLS SENDTO CANVM2 TOOLS REDPRINT GET SG24xxxx PACKAGE
(Canadian users only)
```

To get BookManager BOOKs of redbooks, type the following command:

```
TOOLCAT REDBOOKS
```

To get lists of redbooks:

```
TOOLS SENDTO USDIST MKTTOOLS MKTTOOLS GET ITSOCAT TXT
TOOLS SENDTO USDIST MKTTOOLS MKTTOOLS GET LISTSERV PACKAGE
```

To register for information on workshops, residencies, and redbooks:

```
TOOLS SENDTO WTSCPOK TOOLS ZDISK GET ITSOREGI 1996
```

For a list of product area specialists in the ITSO:

```
TOOLS SENDTO WTSCPOK TOOLS ZDISK GET ORGCARD PACKAGE
```

❏ **Redbooks Home Page on the World Wide Web**

```
http://w3.itso.ibm.com/redbooks
```

❏ **IBM Direct Publications Catalog on the World Wide Web**

```
http://www.elink.ibmlink.ibm.com/pbl/pbl
```

IBM employees may obtain LIST3820s of redbooks from this page.

❏ **REDBOOKS category on INEWS**

❏ **Online** — send orders to: USIB6FPL at IBMMAIL or DKIB-MBSH at IBMMAIL

❏ **Internet Listserver**

With an Internet e-mail address, anyone can subscribe to an IBM Announcement Listserver. To initiate the service, send an e-mail note to announce@webster.ibmlink.ibm.com with the keyword subscribe in the body of the note (leave the subject line blank). A category form and detailed instructions will be sent to you.

How Customers Can Get ITSO Redbooks

Customers may request ITSO deliverables (redbooks, BookManager BOOKs, and CD-ROMs) and information about redbooks, workshops, and residencies in the following ways:

❑ **Online Orders** (Do not send credit card information over the Internet) — send orders to:

	IBMMAIL	Internet
In United States:	usib6fpl at ibmmail	usib6fpl@ibmmail.com
In Canada:	caibmbkz at ibmmail	lmannix@vnet.ibm.com
Outside North America:	dkibmbsh at ibmmail	bookshop@dk.ibm.com

❑ **Telephone orders**

United States (toll free)	1-800-879-2755
Canada (toll free)	1-800-IBM-4YOU
Outside North America	(long distance charges apply)

(+45) 4810 -1320 - Danish	(+45) 4810-1020 - German
(+45) 4810-1420 - Dutch	(+45) 4810-1620 - Italian
(+45) 4810-1540 - English	(+45) 4810-1270 - Norwegian
(+45) 4810-1670 - Finnish	(+45) 4810-1120 - Spanish
(+45) 4810-1220 - French	(+45) 4810-1170 - Swedish

❑ **Mail Orders** — send orders to:

IBM Publications	IBM Publications	IBM Direct Services
Publicatiotzns Customer Support	144-4th Avenue, S.W.	Sortemosevej 21
P.O. Box 29570	Calgary, Alberta T2P 3N5	DK-3450 Aller⁄d
Raleigh, NC 27626-0570	Canada	Denmark
USA		

❑ **Fax** — send orders to:

United States (toll free)	1-800-445-9269

Canada	1-403-267-4455
Outside North America	(+45) 48 14 2207 (long distance charge)

❑ **1-800-IBM-4FAX (United States) or (+1)001-408-256-5422 (Outside USA)** — ask for:

Index # 4421 Abstracts of new redbooks
Index # 4422 IBM redbooks
Index # 4420 Redbooks for last six months

❑ **Direct Services** - send note to softwareshop@vnet.ibm.com

❑ **On the World Wide Web**

Redbooks Home Page http://www.redbooks.ibm.com

IBM Direct Publications Catalog http://www.elink.ibmlink.ibm.com/pbl/pbl

❑ **Internet Listserver**

With an Internet e-mail address, anyone can subscribe to an IBM Announcement Listserver. To initiate the service, send an e-mail note to announce@webster.ibmlink.ibm.com with the keyword subscribe in the body of the note (leave the subject line blank).

IBM Redbook Order Form

Please send me the following:

Title	Order Number	Quantity

First Name _____ **Last Name** _____

Company _____

Address _____

City _____ **Postal Code** _____ **Country** _____

Telephone number _____ **Telefax number** _____

VAT number _____

❐ **Invoice to customer number** _____

❐ **Credit card number** _____

Credit card expiration date _____ **Card issued to** _____

Signature _____

We accept American Express, Diners, Eurocard, Master Card, and Visa. Payment by credit card not available in all countries. Signature mandatory for credit card payment.

DO NOT SEND CREDIT CARD INFORMATION OVER THE INTERNET.

Glossary

A

attribute. An alternative name for *variable*.

associations. Affinities between items in *transactions* that are discovered as the result of *associations discovery*. Associations are expressed as *association rules*.

associations discovery. Data mining technique for discovering *associations*. Its aim is to find *items* in a *transaction* that imply the presence of other items in the same transaction.

association rule. A rule that expresses the affinity between the presence of certain items in a transaction and the presence of other items in the same transaction. The general form of an association rule is X1, X2,... => Y1, Y2....An example is A => B, that is, if A exists in a transaction, then B also exists. See also support factor and confidence factor.

B

back propagation. A general-purpose, *supervised learning* algorithm used by many *neural networks*. Back propagation networks are feed-forward, multi-layer networks that use a *supervised learning* algorithm to adjust the internal connection weights.

back propagation neural network. A *neural network* that uses *back propagation*. The most popular form of neural networks.

business intelligence. General term covering all processes, techniques, and tools that support business decision making based on information technology.

C

categorical variable. A *variable* whose values do not have any relationship among them. The values are useful only as labels. For example, *car-type*, where the possible values are Ford, Nissan, and Lincoln. Sometimes called a *nominal variable*.

classification. A specialization of *predictive modelling* for assigning a class identity to a *record* in a database. The assigned class identity is one from a set of previously known class identities and is based on *variables* within the record. For example, classification could be used to assign a class identity of "Stay" or "Leave" to a database of credit card client records. See *value prediction*.

classification model. A model produced by the *classification* data mining operation. See *predictive modeling*.

cluster. An alternative name for a database *segment*.

clustering. An alternative name for *database segmentation*.

column. An alternative name for *variable*.

commoditization. The trend by which goods and services become so alike that they are increasingly difficult to differentiate.

competitive intelligence. Process of discovering a competitor's strategic decisions or business area characteristics, using quantitative analysis techniques applied to data and information, obtained through legal means, regarding the chosen competitor or business area.

confidence factor. Given an *association rule* A => B, the number of *records* in which B occurs along with A as a percentage of all records in which A occurs, with or without B. The factor indicates the strength of the affinity between the two *items*. See *support factor*.

continuous variable. A variable whose values can take on a subset of real numbers. For example, income or temperature.

D

data mining. The process of extracting previously unknown, valid, and actionable information from large databases and then using the information to inform crucial business decisions.

data mining application. A computer application that uses a *data mining tool* in combination with related technologies such as *exploratory data analysis*, database management, and a graphical user interface.

data mining operation. One of a set of broad strategies for the use of data mining to solve business problems, for example, *database segmentation*.

data mining service. A service in support of a data mining project, ranging from *data mining tool* installation to *business intelligence* consultancy.

data mining technique. A specific implementation of a data mining algorithm in support of one of the *data mining operations*, for example, neural clustering.

data mining tool. A software component for data mining, typically including data preprocessing, one or more mining algorithms, and specialized facilities for visualization of data mining results.

data warehouse. A subject-oriented, documented, integrated, and time-dimensioned collection of data that is used to inform crucial business decisions.

database segmentation. A data mining operation to partition a database into *segments*. The partitioning can be based on one or more *variables* within the records. Segments should have an internal *homogeneity* and a high external *heterogeneity*. Database segmentation is an example of *unsupervised learning*.

decision tree. A group of *nodes* and *leaves* linked together to represent a set of rules followed by a *classification* algorithm in its assignment of class identities to database records.

demographic data. Data related to personal characteristics, for example, age, gender, and number of children.

deviation detection. A data mining operation to detect *outliers* in databases and determine their nature and cause.

dimension. An alternative name for *variable*.

discretization. The act of assigning a set of discrete values to a *continuous variable*. For example, the continuous variable *income*, could be discretized into a new variable called *income-group* with values of 1, 2, and so on to correspond to original income values of $10,000, $20,000 and so on.

E

expert system. A decision support system based on the coding of human expertise in the form if-then-else rules and the interpretation of these rules by a generalized computer program.

exploratory data analysis. A general term covering any data analysis to investigate deep-seated data contents and/or structure, typically using techniques from statistics and OLAP but excluding data mining operations and techniques.

F

feature. An alternative name for *variable*.

field. An alternative name for *variable*.

H

heterogeneity. The degree of dissimilarity (between segments). The opposite of *homogeneity*.

hidden layer. A set of *processing units* in a neural network, positioned between the input and output layers and used to calculate the network output.

homogeneity. The degree of similarity (between segments). The opposite of *heterogeneity*.

I

item. A subpart of a *transaction* that is uniquely identifiable, typically by a record key such as a universal product code (UPC) or customer number.

K

Kohonen feature map. A *neural network* model composed of *processing units* arranged in an input layer and an output layer. All processors in the input layer are connected to each processor in the output layer. The learning algorithm used involves competition between units for each input pattern and the declaration of a winning unit. Used in neural segmentation to partition a database

into *segments*.

L

leaf. The part of a *decision tree* that represents an end-point at which records are collected.

learning algorithm. A set of well-defined rules used during the *training* process to build a *predictive model*.

link analysis. A data mining operation to detect affinities between *items* both within and between *transactions*, possibly over time. Link analysis includes the *associations discovery, sequential pattern discovery,* and *similar time sequence discovery* data mining techniques.

M

metadata. Data that describes the characteristics of *variables*, for example, a column in a database table can be described by the metadata entries of length and data type.

N

neural induction. A method of developing a *predictive model* or a *classification model* using a *neural network* and a *supervised learning* algorithm.

neural network. A computing model based on the architecture of the brain consisting of multiple simple *processing units* connected by adaptive weights. A collection of *processing units* and adaptive connections that is designed to perform a specific processing function. A neural network is used for pattern recognition, particularly for *classification*, but also for other tasks that involve approximation such as *predictive modeling*.

node. The part of a *decision tree* that represents a testing of the value of an associated *variable*. On the basis of the different values of the *variable*, the tree will potentially branch out to other nodes, and so on.

nominal variable. An alternative name for a *categorical variable*.

noisy data. Data with missing or invalid values. See *outliers*.

O

OLAP. An extension of the relational database paradigm to support business modeling. It takes the form of a number of rules designed to facilitate fast and easy access to the data for purposes of management information and decision support.

outliers. Variables or records which have values that do not conform to some expected norm. Outliers can be good or bad: good outliers indicate potentially valuable information (an unusually high-valued or fraudulent transaction), and bad outliers indicate *noisy data*.

overfitting. The phenomenon by which *predictive models* learn too well the detailed patterns in the input data during the *training process* and are therefore unable to make good generalizations about new input data. Also called *overtraining*.

overtraining. An alternative name for *overfitting*

P

predictive modeling. A data mining operation that uses the contents of a database of known cases to generate a model that can help to predict a class or value associated with new, unseen cases. Has two specializations: *classifi-*

cation and *value prediction*.

processing unit. A processing unit in a neural network used to calculate an output value by summing all incoming values multiplied by their respective adaptive connection weights.

psychographic data. Data related to personal behavior, for example, favorite kind of music, preferred vacation locations, and average weekly expenses on groceries.

Q

quantile. One of a finite number of non-overlapping sub-ranges or intervals, each of which is represented by an assigned value.

quartile. One of four *quantiles*.

R

radial basis function. Used in the data mining technique that predicts values. Represents a function of the distance or the radius from a particular point. Used to build up approximations to more complex functions.

record. A collection of data values all belonging to a particular instance or occurrence, as for instance, to the same *transaction* or to the same individual. In database terminology, record is synonymous with row. See *variable*.

rule. An alternative name for *association rule*.

rule body. Given an *association rule* X => Y, X is the rule body.

rule head. Given an *association rule* X => Y, Y is the rule body. Represents the derived items detected by an associations algorithm.

S

segment. A sub-population of *records* within a database which all have similar characteristics based on similarity between the values of their *variables*.

segmentation. An alternative name of *database segmentation*.

self-organizing feature map. See *Kohonen feature map*.

sequential pattern discovery. A data mining technique to discover *associations* between *transactions* over time.

sequential patterns. *Associations* between *transactions* such that the presence of one set of *items* is followed by another set of items in a database of transactions over a period of time.

similar time sequence discovery. A data mining technique to discover *associations* between a series of related *transactions* over time.

supervised learning. A *learning algorithm* that requires input and resulting output pairs to be presented to the network during the *training process*. *Back propagation*, for example, used supervised learning and makes adjustments during training so that the value computed by the neural network will approach the actual supplied value as the network learns from the data presented. Used in the data mining techniques provided for *classification* and *value prediction*. See *unsupervised learning*.

support factor. Given an *association rule* A => B, the number of *records* in which this rule occurs as a percentage of all records in the database. The factor indicates the relative frequency with which the rule occurs in the data. See *confidence factor*.

T

taxonomy. A classification assigning hierarchies to related *items*. The taxonomy relation defines item categories for each level of the hierarchy. An example is a product hierarchy, for example, where apple would be in the fruit category, which in turn is part of the produce category, and so on.

training process. The process of developing a model which understands a data source. In neural networks, the process of adjusting the connection weights in a neural network under the control of a *learning algorithm*.

transaction. A set of *items* or events that are linked by a common key value, for example, where a store ID, EPOS terminal number, and transaction sequence number defines the key value for a customer transaction at a retail store.

tree induction. A method for building a *classification* model in the form of a binary *decision tree*. Each interior *node* of this binary decision tree tests an *attribute* of a *record*.

U

unsupervised learning. A *learning algorithm* that required only input data to be present in the data source during the *training process*. No target output is provided; instead, the desired output is discovered during the mining run. *Kohonen feature maps* use unsupervised learning. See *supervised learning*.

V

value prediction. A specialization of *predictive modelling* for assigning a value or propensity to a *record* in a database. The assigned value or propensity is based on *attributes* within the record.

For example, value prediction could be used to assign a propensity to respond to a mailing campaign to records in a prospects database. See *classification*.

variable. A data *item* within a *record* which represents some characteristic of the instance described by the record. For example, credit-limit and income could be items in a customer record. Some alternative names are *attribute*, *feature*, *field*, *column*, and *dimension*. See *record*. In database terminology, variable is synonymous with *column*.

visualization technique. A technique by which to graphically display data. Helps the user in understanding the structure and meaning of the discovered information contained in the data.

List of Abbreviations

API	application programming interface
ATM	automatic teller machine
BT	British Telecom
CRM	customer relationship management
CVA	customer vulnerability analysis
DDA	demand deposit account
DIS	data interpretation system
EDA	exploratory data analysis
EIS	Executive Information System
FAMS	fraud and abuse management system
FBE	full blood examination
GDP	gross domestic product
GP	general practitioner
GUI	graphical user interface
HELOC	home equity line of credit
HIC	Health Insurance Commission
IBM	International Business Machines Corporation
ID	identifier
IDS	Intelligent Decision Server
IMS	information management system
ISU	industry solution unit
IT	information technology
ITSO	International Technical Support Organization
KDD	knowledge discovery in databases
MBA	(1) market basket analysis (2) multiple biochemical analysis
MDA	multidimensional data analysis
MDD	Multidimensional database
MPP	massively parallel processor
NBA	National Basketball Association
ODBC	open data base connectivity
OJ	orange juice
OECD	Organization for Economic Cooperation and Development
OLAP	online analytical processing
OLTP	online transaction processing
PC	personal computer
PEI	pathology episode initiation
POS	point of sale
RBF	radial basis function
ROI	return on investment
RPC	remote procedure call
ROLAP	relational online analytical processing
SMP	symmetric multiprocessor
SQL	structured query language
TPC	Transaction Processing Council
UDP	user defined program
UPC	universal product code
VCR	video cassette recorder
Web	World Wide Web
WPIL	World Patent Index Latest

Index

Numerics

Muller, Philippe 105
Niagara 61
Nii, P 89
Onassis, Aristotle 3
overestimate 89
Pentagon 61
risk 125
technology 89
underestimate 89

R

radial basis function 77
RBF, See radial basis function
Redbrick 93
REPSOL 33
response fit 118
response model 117
retail industry and data mining
    applications 162
    cleanliness of POS data 49
    competitive price prediction 33
    customer segmentation 28
    customer vulnerability analysis 31, 45–58
    fraud application 100
    loyalty cards 28
    POS fraud detection 34
    sales trends analysis 69
    store promotion design 30
    telesales promotions 27
RetailQuery 162
return on investment, See cost-benefit analysis
Right Information Systems 91
ROI, See cost-benefit analysis
roles 44
Rosenblatt, Frank 14
RS Components 27
rule body 81
rule head 81

S

sampling 49, 94, 98
SAS Institute Inc. 91
SAS System 91
scalability
    Intelligent Miner 142, 145
    limitations of current tools 98
    requirements for 98

scatterplot 50, 66, 87
Schwab 85 Co., Charles 36
scoring 65
Scout 31
SE-Learn / SE-Classify 101
sensitivity analysis, See input sensitivity analysis
sequential pattern discovery
    definition 83
    example 84, 85
    Intelligent Miner 143
    positioning within data mining approaches 62
    usage considerations 85
shelf life 48
SHL Systemhouse 102
ShopKo 30
siftware 90
Silicon Graphics Inc. 91
similar time sequence discovery
    and margin for error 86
    and mismatch gap 86
    definition 85
    Intelligent Miner 143
    positioning within data mining approaches 62
    usage considerations 86
Simon Fraser University 91
single-task tools 92
skills 134, 136
Solomon 101
SPSS 93
Stanford University 91
statistics
    and deviation detection 88
    contrasted with data mining 17
    positioning within data mining approaches 62
    use during data preprocessing 49, 54
SunGlass Hut 6
supervised learning 64, 70
supplementary variable 48
support factor 81, 83, 110, 111
Surf-Aid 166
Sybase 93, 102, 142
Syllogic International B.V. 101
symbol mapping 94

T

target marketing, See database marketing
Technology Watch 165